Revised and Expanded Edition

SHARING
the Faith
WITH
Your Child

From Birth to Age Four

PHYLLIS CHANDLER, JOAN BURNEY,
AND MARY KAY LEATHERMAN

Liguori

Imprimi Potest:
Thomas D. Picton, C.Ss.R.
Provincial, Denver Province
The Redemptorists

Imprimatur:
Most Reverend Robert J. Hermann
Auxiliary Bishop
Archdiocese of St. Louis

978-0-7648-1523-2
Library of Congress Card Number: 2006932979

© 2006, Liguori Publications
Printed in the United States of America
15 16 17 18 19 / 9 8 7 6 5

Compliant with *The Roman Missal*, third edition.

Liguori Publications, a nonprofit corporation, is an apostolate of the Redemptorists. To learn more about the Redemptorists, visit Redemptorists.com.

Table of Contents

Raising Children in Today's World

To the Parents of a New Child

"Whoever welcomes one such child in my name welcomes me, and whoever welcomes me welcomes not me but the one who sent me."

MARK 9:37

ONE OF THE GREATEST calls to holiness is the role of parenting. Though it is not a sacrament, it is certainly a significant ministry that mirrors the relationship between God and the Church. As you give selflessly to your child daily, you are holy. Just as a wedding ring is a sign of the sacrament of marriage, an apron or a briefcase is truly a sign of your holiness as a parent.

As overwhelming as it may seem, from the moment of conception your child depends on you for all of his or her needs. After birth, you nourish your baby with food and provide a safe, comfortable home. You meet your child's every need. Christ tells us, "for I was hungry and you gave me food, I was thirsty and you gave me something to drink…I was naked and you gave me clothing, I was sick and you took care of me" (Matthew 25:35–36). You are serving Christ by serving your child. Others may help, but you accept the task as your privilege and responsibility. God has called you to care for this unique child. You are chosen. You are holy.

The same is true of your child's faith development. You nurture his or her spiritual growth just as you do the physical. You do this through the day-by-day experiences your child has within your family.

As a parent, you have a special opportunity to welcome Jesus in this child. Through you, more than through anyone else, God's love will be communicated to your child. You are your child's first sense of God. Through your guidance, your son or daughter will come to know the qualities Jesus shared with us in his words and example. In return, your child will help you grow in faith just as Jesus would help you if he lived in your home.

This book has been written to help you welcome your child into your life, your home, and your faith. It deals with the day-to-day living that goes into faith development from birth to age four. Some of what you find here you may use at once. Some of it you may want to come back to and reread in the months and years ahead. Use this book to share life and faith with your child.

Although this book is primarily for Catholic parents, much of it can be helpful to parents who belong to other Christian traditions and other faiths. If you are not a Catholic but are married to one, this book can help you understand your and your spouse's roles in your children's faith development.

Becoming Parents

1
Welcoming Your Child

"A baby is an inestimable blessing and bother."

MARK TWAIN

THE BIRTH OF A CHILD is a major event in the life of any family. Whether it is your first child or your fifth, you will experience many emotions as you develop your expectations and hopes about being a mother or father. Your feelings may range from joy and excitement to apprehension and fear. There may be times when you look upon the coming event as anything but a blessing. These feelings are a normal part of the process of preparing to become a parent.

Parents are a unique and special part of God's plan. A child is a new life flowing from your love relationship. A child is also a sharing of God's love in the process of creation. As a parent you share intimately in the initial development of God's gift of life.

You will experience trying times and exciting times as you prepare to become a parent. Knowing the importance of your mission can help you deal with these feelings. It is worth remembering your call to holiness on days when you feel overwhelmed. Remaining mindful of this reality through all of your daily routines and acts of self-giving will transform your attitude into Christ's attitude of love. Soon the ordinary tasks become sacred rituals.

Your relationship with your baby begins long before birth. This preparation period is a particularly important time for you as a parent, especially if this child is your first. The variety of emotions you feel are normal.

Very early, you as a parent-to-be form images about yourself as a parent, about your spouse as a parent, and about the child you will have. This image-forming helps you prepare for the changes about to occur in your life. Your images will be shaped by your own experience—especially your childhood—and what you have been taught and believe a parent should be. Your images will be uniquely yours, just as you and your spouse are unique.

Bonding

As you and your baby come to know each other, you will begin to value one another's unique traits and develop a special, one-of-a-kind relationship. This process is called bonding, or attachment. A child needs someone to trust regarding his or her needs for love and security. Especially in the first months of life, a child needs to know that those needs will be met.

You welcome Jesus in your child each time you respond to such needs. At the same time, the child begins to know a loving and caring God through your love and care.

By the time he or she begins school at about age five, much of what your child will know in any area has already been learned, and you, as parent, will have been the main teacher. No one will ever influence your child's development as much as you do in these early years. This includes religious development. If you are a religious family, your child will acquire a good foundation for religion during these years. Proverbs 22:6 notes:

> *"Train children in the right way,*
> *and when old, they will not stray."*

Perfection Is Not a Human Attribute

Of course, you will not be the perfect parent. No one is. Every parent experiences negative feelings from time to time, and no parent is able to respond to every child's needs.

Remember, negative feelings are normal. These feelings occur especially when your own needs aren't being met or when you are tired or frustrated. Caring for small children all day with no adult contact can be frustrating. Middle-of-the-night feedings are rarely times of great joy. It is important that you take care of yourself, both physically and emotionally, for your own sake as well as that of your child. It helps during these times to retain your sense of humor and to remember that your child will grow up.

Relationships Change

A new child brings about an adjustment of relationships. This tiny person will bring an added dimension to the love you and your spouse have for one another. You will share a sense of awe and wonder at the creative power of God at work in your lives.

But you may also find it difficult to make enough time for yourselves as a couple. Work at making that time. A satisfactory relationship with your spouse should not take second place to your concern for your child. Your child will learn about love and service from the way you talk, touch, look at, and laugh with each other. Your relationship with your spouse will be the foundation for your child's relationship with others and with God.

As the saying has it, "The best thing a father can do for his child is to love the child's mother." That's good advice for mothers, too.

Even if you already have children, welcoming a new child will be special and different. Because you are constantly in the process of "becoming," of growing and learning, each of your children will enter a different family. No two babies are exactly alike, so the whole relationship will be a new experience. You learn about parenting all over again no matter how many children you already have.

Advice All Around

There are several secrets to surviving the experience of parenthood. One secret is to take advantage of the "experts." Learn all you can from them about child development. Becoming knowledgeable will give you flexibility and self-confidence. It will not produce perfect children, because even the most normal, healthy child is sometimes difficult. But being informed will help you cope.

There are many resources available today on how to raise healthy, well-adjusted children. In addition to books, many CDs, DVDs, and websites can advise you on the huge task of raising your child today. Advice can often be confusing because "experts" disagree with each other. You may wonder, "How can I raise my child properly if even the experts disagree?"

The best solution is to hear and read what the experts say, discuss the problems with other parents you respect, then trust in your own abilities and instincts. Don't try to pattern your family after somebody else's idea of a "perfect" family. You alone know your situation and the kinds of things that work for you and for your children. Develop your own style and you will do a good job.

Recognize your uniqueness; be exactly who and what you are. Remember: as a parent you are co-creator with God. God calls us, encourages us, and challenges us as parents. God will support you in this joyous task. Ask God for guidance and pray daily for your children. You will find that there is no better way to approach the mystery of God than to be involved in the development and growth of children.

2
The Family as Domestic Church

"You are the bows from which your children
as living arrows are sent forth...."

KAHLIL GIBRAN

AS A NEW PARENT, you have so many decisions to make. What kind of diapers will you use? Will you breastfeed? Will one of you be able to stay home with your baby or will you have to make a decision regarding daycare? These decisions can become overwhelming, especially when you stop to consider, "I am making decisions that will affect this child's life."

One important decision that you will make, whether deliberately or not, is that of raising your child in a religious family. This decision for your child will most certainly impact your own faith life as well as that of your child. Daily routines and traditions in the home create a beautiful net of faith that supports your child as he or she grows.

Baptism Is the First Step

The first step of initiation into the Catholic Church is the sacrament of baptism. If you choose this for your child, you will find that the beauty of this sacrament is that it often rekindles the faith of adults who may have strayed from religious practices for one reason or another. How wonderful that a small child raises the bar for us in so many ways!

Baptism makes us sharers in God's own life and welcomes us into his family. The Greek word baptizo means "to plunge." How coincidental is it that baptism is a plunging into new life on so many levels. The promise of new life is one that Jesus is constantly giving us. This "paschal" mystery of baptism is a dying of one life that must take place in order for new life to unfold.

Programs of preparation for baptism are offered in most parishes. Talk to your pastor approximately two months before you wish to celebrate your child's baptism to allow time for preparation and instruction. In many parishes, baptisms take place in the parish church at Sunday Mass. In this way, family, friends, and church members can welcome your child into the faith community.

After baptism, your family becomes the center of your child's religious experience. This includes attendance at Mass, and prayers at meals and bedtime. If you want your child to take religion seriously, he or she must see that you value prayer and worship in your own lives. These practices, however, are not guarantees of full spiritual development even for a small child.

A Faith Lived in the Home

One of the great things about us as God's people is that we grow in our knowledge of spiritual realities. As the Second Vatican Council stated, "There is a growth in insight into the realities and words that are being passed on" (Dogmatic Constitution on Divine Revelation, 8). A good case of such growth is Vatican II's own insight into family: "In what might be regarded as the domestic Church, the parents, by word and example, are the first heralds of the faith with regard to their children" (Dogmatic Constitution on the Church, 11).

Just as the family is the basic unit of society, it is also the basic unit of the Church. The domestic Church is a setting where Christians can share with one another what Jesus lived and taught us. It is within the sacrament of your marriage and your vocation of parenthood that your child first comes to know God. Within a family, the members can experience the power of God's love. The caring of the family unit can be brought into the parish and the community. In the domestic Church parents are the primary religious educators. No one else—priests, teachers or friends—can influence the development of religious values as can a parent. By action or omission, your child learns far more from you than from anyone else.

The loving relationship between you and your child accounts for this powerful influence. You are the most important person in your child's life, and it will be your values and examples that he or she will most likely imitate.

The meaning of God's love is learned through loving relationships with family members. Forgiveness within the family teaches God's forgiving love. Punishment by parents teaches children to fear a punishing God. A child learns religion by being a part of a family that practices Christian values in its everyday life.

Parish programs such as preschool religious education can support efforts to develop your child's fundamentals of spirituality, but they cannot replace your influence. Parish early childhood programs should enrich and reinforce experiences in Christian families. They should be supplements, rather than substitutes, for a faith lived in the home.

You begin your involvement in your child's growth in faith through your preparation for and participation in baptism. But even before that, you are your child's primary religious educator. Primary means "first." Primary also means "most important." You are both!

3
Understanding How Your Child Learns

"All healthy children begin with an enormous interest in the world about them, a freshness and luminosity of vision. A four-year-old child marveling at the blurred ribbons of color in a grease puddle bends closer: 'It's a dead rainbow!' A five-year-old child whose foot has fallen asleep wriggles in amazement: 'My toes feel like ginger ale!'"

FREDELLE MAYNARD

CHILDREN LEARN ABOUT GOD and develop religious faith by seeing, feeling, and hearing. How they do this is fascinating, and it will help you to know the different stages of development your child will go through.

It was by carefully observing his own children that Swiss psychologist Jean Piaget developed his theory about children's intellectual development. Children, according to Piaget, are born with a desire to know, a curiosity about the world that leads them to learn. But, said Piaget, children do not learn in the same way adults do. How do children learn? Here are examples of the stages they go through.

Babies: Preoccupied with Self

The only world that exists for a baby is the world of experience—what the infant feels, sees, hears, tastes, etc. The baby is totally preoccupied with self. There is no concern for you or for others. You exist only to meet his or her demands for food, warmth, and love. Your baby assumes that he or she owns you and controls your actions.

The infant believes he or she is the center of the world and everything revolves around this center. This perception, though not accurate, is normal and necessary. It is the only way a baby comprehends. Experience will bring about a more realistic view. At this point, because a baby knows only experience, the message that the world is good must come from your care and love.

All the things in an infant's world—including you—exist for that infant only when he or she can see, hear, smell, or touch them.

By the time the child is a year old, however, an image of things exists in his or her mind. Along with that image is the realization that things, including you, come and go. It is then that your child may become upset when you leave the room or a stranger picks him up. A child may want only Mom and no one else, not even Dad. This can be a trying time, but it is temporary. The child soon learns that Mom will come back and also learns to trust others.

Ages Three and Four: Egocentric

Children are still "egocentric" at ages three and four. Some new awareness exists of the rights and needs of others, but these children are still convinced that everyone should see things their way. If the child wants a truck, a friend should let her have it. The concept of equal rights is beyond your child's ability. This is not selfishness; it is simply the level at which the child is functioning.

Children below age five usually see objects in terms of one characteristic or relationship. Someone who is their "friend" cannot be another person's friend at the same time. Objects are categorized by shape or color but not both. The person who is "Daddy" to a little girl cannot be husband, brother, or son to others.

As children come into contact with their environment, the ability to understand and "make sense" of things gradually expands and new relationships appear. The bits and pieces of information gathered through thousands of individual experiences fall into place. Concepts emerge and are applied to new and varied situations.

Learning by Doing and Playing

Learning takes place by doing, so your child needs experiences, not explanations. Walking through fallen leaves teaches about seasons. Pouring water from one container to another teaches weight, volume, and measurement. Smiles and hugs teach love. Visits with relatives teach family relationships.

Play is the way by which children manipulate their world so that it makes sense. Play may be "fun," but it is also the serious business of learning. As children play, they often pretend to be animals or other persons. This is how they "try on" what it will be like for them to have a new experience (a baby in the family, a trip to the hospital) or what it was like in the past (being a baby, yesterday's trip to the zoo). Play is necessary to growth and development.

Children's Concepts of Right and Wrong

Children's limited experience and understanding make it impossible for them to have adult concepts of right and wrong. For example, children often take things they would like to have, including items on the shelves of stores. This is not "stealing" as we know it. If they wish they had a new tricycle and tell their friends they got one, they are not "lying" as we understand a lie. To small children, "right" is what makes them happy or what pleases people who are important to them. "Wrong" is what makes children unhappy or upsets parents. Our adult concepts of sin, justice, or social responsibility are impossible for small children to understand. These adult understandings will develop as the child matures.

This chapter is not a complete description of the learning process of early childhood; it merely provides some key characteristics to help you understand that process. Chapter 18 will discuss the moral dimension of personal development more fully.

4
Modeling Faith for Your Child

"...If you could creep into your children's minds while they are saying their night prayers and see the visual image of God they are praying to, you would find your own face there. You are the only way your children can relate to God in their early years."

LARSEN AND GALVIN

WHAT IS YOUR IMAGE OF GOD? As a parent, one of your tasks is to bring God's presence into the life experiences of your child. But who is the God you want your child to learn about? Is your God a loving father? Or is God a judge? a punisher? Is your God tender and caring, like a mother? Or strict and demanding, like a lawmaker? What is your image of God? Whatever your answer, that is the God that you will share with your child.

The most important image of God is one we frequently encounter in Scripture and theology. In the First Letter of John (4:8) we read: "Whoever does not love does not know God, for God is love." It does not say "God loves us if we are good." It does not say "God is loving." It says: "God IS love." Being loved, learning to love others, and learning about God are so closely interwoven that they are a single process. This process takes place between you and your child.

Love Is the Best Teacher

Therefore, it is love that best teaches children about God. Indeed, Saint John's words, "Whoever does not love does not know God," tell us that experiencing love is absolutely necessary to a child's faith. By feeling and seeing and being touched by your love—a love that is constant, forgiving, unconditional, and lasting—your child will come to understand God.

Author Mary Reed Newland points out: "Which word does a small child understand first—love or God? The word love, of course, because being loved is the most important thing in his life." By being loved, your child will learn to love. This is your major task as a parent. Trusting you, your child will learn to trust others. You are the center of his or her growing circle of awareness.

Love is shown in more ways than by hugs and kisses. It is communicated through playing games of peek-a-boo, reading bedtime stories, waiting out a dozen attempts to "do it myself," admiring a picture, sharing a snack, and taking an evening walk. The image of God comes through in every experience a child has with a loving parent.

As they grow and mature, children watch and imitate their parents' attitudes and behavior. "The" way to do things will be the way Mom and Dad do them. Your child will want to share your faith values. From your interpretation of life—through example, as well as through spoken and unspoken messages—your child will learn about God.

5
Fostering Your Marriage and Yourself

Morgan watched as her mother put on a new dress and brushed her hair. "Are we going to a party? I'll go get my party dress." The four-year-old was devastated to tears when she discovered that her mother and father were going out for their anniversary without her.

AT FIRST GLANCE, this appears to be a sad story of exclusion and grief, but with a deeper look at this world, you might see how fortunate this little girl is to have parents who foster their marriage. This young child's awareness of her mother and father's love for each other, evident here in measures they take to spend time alone, are very important. As Morgan's parents model a healthy example of marriage, Morgan begins to form her own views on marriage that will be beneficial to her when she becomes an adult.

Even though you might view effective parenting as a completely selfless ministry, the reality is that you will best parent if you first take care of yourself and your marriage, physically, emotionally and spiritually. When a marriage is Christ-centered and thriving rather than just surviving, a mother and father can give much more to the family and each individual child. Little Morgan may have had one bad day as a four-year-old, but she will grow up secure in her parent's love for each other.

Likewise, a single parent must attend to his or her own spiritual, emotional and physical health in order to give the children what they need in those areas. A drained parent, on any of those levels, cannot give with the same heart and may either neglect or over-indulge children as a result. A beautiful balance has always been God's plan in your calling to be a parent.

Consequences of the Condition of Your Marriage

The positive condition of your marriage is a nice secure net for your children and a good model. Your children watch you in your marriage on good days and on bad days.

When a child feels secure about her parents' relationship, she is free to focus on being a child. When a child feels insecure about her parents' relationship, she often feels anxiety and concern for the very people who should be protecting her from such an environment.

Balancing life can be a challenge for any couple. This is a given fact. Demands from work, extended family, daily tasks, and children's needs all seem to tug at a mother and father. Often the marriage is put on the back burner in what many mistake as the right thing to do. Often they think the marriage will "take care of itself" as they take care of everything else.

The divorce rate today is evidence of many neglected marriages, though it is easy to see how that slow division might take place. One mother explains, "When the day is over, I have given and given. I am too tired to give anymore...my husband should understand that." One father adds, "When I am at work all day, I feel guilty that I am not around my kids. When I get home, I want to spend that time with them before I spend time with my wife." It is easy to see how and why parents sometimes neglect taking the time to nurture their marriage.

Regardless, parents need to make a conscious effort to protect their marriage. So many people think that a good marriage should just "happen," without much attention or effort. But people who have good marriages have worked at that union. The work begins with a daily dialogue between spouses. When parents consistently monitor the "temperature" of their marriage, they are saying that it is important.

A simple question each day to your spouse, "What do you need from me?" can mark the difference between a good marriage and a shaky one. The question implies that you want to do something for the other. Many marriages struggle through the years as each spouse wonders the opposite: "What is my spouse going to do for me today?" A beautiful energy comes from reversing that mindset. "Can I pick up milk on the way home from work so you don't have to take the kids out in the rain?" "Can I make you a lunch so that you can get caught up during the lunch hour rather than go out to eat?"

In making a conscious decision to focus on the marriage, parents are not neglecting their children. This is not selfish on the part of a mother and father; it is a healthy priority.

Most people are not familiar with the concept "protecting your marriage," but the truth is many parts of our society can attack the stability of your union with your spouse. When a mother and father work toward taking time for each other, a child learns that marriage is important. The hope is that he or she will carry that knowledge into his or her own sacramental commitment to another someday.

Physical Balance

Exercise can energize you and make you feel good about yourself. Just read any of the health magazines out today.

In addition to impacting your own physical well-being and mood, exercise and eating habits impact your child, whose strongest example of how to tend to his or her physical well-being is you. The child who see his or her parent lying on the couch watching TV every night may adopt these same habits in later years.

Of course, finding the time for exercise is difficult for a parent of young children. Many parents become creative as they take their children in strollers or on their backs to get a daily walk in. Eventually, you can look forward to exercising with your children as the children mature. Children can only benefit from parents who take the time to take care of themselves physically and pass on good habits.

Sadly, the headlines today also expose problems in our society regarding poor nutrition and eating habits. Obesity is a major problem in our youth today, which can lead to life-long health problems. Eating disorders are another problem among young people in our image-conscious society. Parents must be aware of the emotional impact when they talk about their own bodies in front of their children. Even very young children can be influenced by a negative comment such as, "I am so fat. I don't like my body."

Balancing Daily Demands

The balancing act continues as we face the many daily demands that get in the way of family time and marriage time. It soon becomes easy to begrudge the calendar and resent our spouse as chores pile up. "Can't he see I need help with laundry?" "Our life is just crazy. We just run from one thing to the next." "Why does her family want to get together all of the time. I can't seem to get a moment to myself."

In addition to praying for God's help for emotional stability, we must keep a daily watch of the events of the day and the impact these have on our marriage and family. All too often we fall into the trap of being Victims to the Calendar. An overly busy life can wear us down, causing us to lose focus and peace. Children who live in the midst of stressful and chaotic schedules believe that this is the only way to live. We are passing on the chaos when we don't model a peaceful, calm home environment.

The challenge is to take control of our lives. One father jokes that he cannot schedule anything outside of work until he "runs it by the committee. The committee is my wife!" Saying no to activities that might be fun but may get in the way of family or marriage time is not only a good idea, it is clearly protecting the sanctity and sanity of the family. Just as great marriages are not "pure luck," good families also come from careful attention and planning.

When couples do not take the time to share with each other about the daily frustrations and joys, a rift begins that can never be good. One husband exclaims, "My wife thinks I read her mind. I didn't know that she had a bad day. Suddenly she is mad at me." Sharing frustrations and concern is one way to prevent a rift in the relationship.

Daily dialogue should include personal interests and activities. One mother said, "If I can just get out of the house for a walk by myself, I feel that I come back renewed." Another father said, "When I joined the men's basketball league in our parish, I realized how much I needed that hour a week." Spouses who encourage each other to take "personal time" and take turns caring for the children will eventually see positive results. Even young children can see when Mom and Dad are happy and take time for themselves.

Some spouses may come to a point where outside help is needed to guide them through emotional conflicts. It is not a sign of weakness to ask for help; it is a sign of concern for your marriage. Counseling can be a wonderful way to foster your marriage.

Spiritual Balance

One father compared his marriage to the ripples in a lake when a rock is thrown into the water. "God is the rock at the center of my life. My marriage is the next ripple. My children the next. My extended family, friends, and then eventually all the other people and events in my day follow that. When God is not the center or my marriage is not important, everything else falls apart. The ripple is broken."

A wife and husband need to explore their faith and spirituality together. Praying with the family at meals and at bedtime is a great way to keep the Lord present. One couple prays in bed right before they go to sleep. "We need to keep Christ present in our marriage daily. We need to place our needs and gratitude before God and each other as a couple. It felt a little silly at first—praying with one another—but now it is a beautiful given in our routine."

A single parent should find balance in his or her life, too: making time to relax with friends, to exercise, to pray, and to pursue hobbies. It is healthy for children to see Mom or Dad making time for good friends or interesting activities.

Being a Family

6
The Changing Role of Family

"God, give us the grace to accept with serenity the things that cannot be changed, courage to change the things which should be changed, and the wisdom to distinguish one from the other."

REINHOLD NIEBUHR

THE SACRAMENT OF MARRIAGE and the vocation of parenthood are as important as ever to Christian parents. The challenge today is to find effective ways of living the sacrament and vocation in the midst of change.

When life does not go the way we think it should, God asks us to handle it the best way we can. With grace. Christ was sentenced to a painful, humiliating death, one he surely did not plan for. He humbly offered that cross up for us. When the structure of our lives or unexpected outcomes disappoint us, we must humbly and positively offer our cross to God.

Traditional family patterns have undergone tremendous change in recent years, but that change does not always have to be seen as bad or wrong, even though for many these changes are disappointing. The traditional family, composed of parents and children with father as breadwinner and mother as full-time homemaker, is now in the minority.

Whatever your family situation, the family you grew up in will remain a strong influence on the kind of family you want to have. You will compare yourself to your mother or father and reflect on your own childhood as you share your child's experience.

Changes Young Families Are Faced With

Changing patterns of family life are creating new experiences for young parents to face. Two of the more prevalent challenging experiences are:

- feelings of isolation
- lack of time

Isolation

Many parents today experience a feeling of isolation as they cope with the day-to-day effort of raising their children. Grandparents and extended family members may not live close by or may be unavailable to offer advice. There may not be anyone with whom to share a child's small but significant accomplishments—that long-awaited first step, a drawing of a rainbow, the first day of school.

In addition, the demands of certain jobs force some families to move frequently and this keeps them from establishing close ties with neighbors or lasting friendships. For many, the feeling of belonging which comes from being rooted in a community is missing. A support system of loving, caring "others" is not always available to share the joy or ease the frustrations that are so much a part of family.

The good news is that support is there; we just need to look for it. At first, parents will need to work to make those connections, but they are present in many communities. A parish is a great place to start making connections with others. The Chamber of Commerce is another good resource and sometimes sponsors programs for families moving to a new community. Finally, the Internet offers quick access to information in a new community.

The effort to connect will be well worth it!

Time

Lack of time is another factor that creates pressure for family members. Coordinating the schedules of four or more persons becomes complicated and hectic. Children are often hurried through music lessons, swim classes, and scout meetings by mothers who have PTA meetings, aerobics, church functions, and dinners to cook for fathers who work late at the office, play golf, and participate in civic and political organizations. Adults and children are so busy doing they have no time to enjoy being.

But we do not have to be victims of time. When we choose to take control of our lives, they become ours. When a situation seems hopeless, we can make the best of it. One family struggled with the fact that Dad's job did not get him home until 8:00 p.m., well past dinner time. Instead of complaining about the situation, the family sat together and had a bowl of ice cream while Dad ate dinner. The point is taking time for each other even if we need to adjust our schedules a bit.

Some Things Unchanged, Some Changes Healthy

Many things about family life remain unchanged. The need to belong, to be part of a family, is still basic to each individual, and most parents feel responsible for nurturing that need to belong. The family is still the place where people receive unconditional love and acceptance.

As for change, the picture is not all bad. Many changes affecting family life are healthy ones with the potential to strengthen families. For example, the greater freedom women have to pursue employment outside the home has brought fathers into a more active role in child-rearing. The opportunity for men to nurture their children has enriched their lives and those of their families. Women are growing in self-esteem as they choose homemaking, a career, or a combination of the two.

Studies are showing that day care, wisely selected, is not a detriment to the parent-child relationship and can have positive effects on many areas of development. Children who see themselves as contributing members of a family are growing up with a more positive sense of worth. And men who previously assumed the entire burden of financial decision-making are suffering less stress by sharing the responsibility with their wives.

The family is not disintegrating. The family is changing. Change may result in better ways to be a family.

Commitment Finds the Way

To be a good parent you don't have to do things the same way your mother and father did them.

In Bringing Religion Home, Mary Theresa Judd identified three qualities of good Christian parents:

1. They know their task is to pass on love and a sense of self-worth to their children.
2. They are prepared for and supported in the task of child-rearing.
3. They recognize the value of a loving family to Christian life.

Essential to the development of these qualities is commitment. It takes commitment to find effective ways to be a family, to share love, to develop trust, to learn how to be a better parent. Each family needs to develop these basic values; they do not come into being by themselves. The amount of time you invest in this effort need not be great. Making the commitment to keep the family a priority is the main thing.

Your commitment to family life should be clear to others. It may require courage to say, "I can't work overtime, my family needs me at home." Or, "We won't be able to attend the party, we planned an evening with our children." If you show that commitment, most of your friends and associates will respect it. You will get support from those who share your values.

The primary purpose of the family is to develop in people the ability to love. The family of today has just as many or more resources to do this as the family of a generation ago.

7
Family Functionality

Isabella held her imaginary phone to her head with her doll in one arm and her hand on her hip. She spoke clearly but firmly to her imaginary husband on the other end of the line, "Fine, but if you are going to be late again, your dinner will be cold and sitting on the counter."

FAMILIES WILL HAVE CONFLICTS, marriages will have problems, and daily altercations will find their ways into the family situations of the day. This is fact. What families decide to do with that conflict is their choice, and an important one at that. Dysfunctional is a buzz word that is overused and even misused today as a label for problems within a family.

"Dysfunction" does not mean problems, but rather, failing to deal with those problems in healthy ways.

Parents enter "parenthood" with tools to deal with problems that were passed on from their family of origin. Tools of communication, conflict resolution, and approaches to tradition and intimacy were learned, positively or negatively, from the parents' own family situation. Whether they like it or not, a mother and father will pass on these tools to their own children.

A healthy couple will engage in a "sorting out" process. Husband and wife must acknowledge and address the good and bad tools that they have carried into the marriage from their past. They need to be open to changing some of the unhealthy habits they have brought to the marriage and family. A wife who comes from a long line of grudge-holders will need to decide if she really wants her children to learn how to be mad for days at a time. A father will have to work at hugging his children if his father never hugged him.

Families will face challenges daily which will test them. The dog ran away. Dad needs to works late. The baby has a fever so one parent will need to stay home from work. The dog ran away again. Mom and Dad have to help Grandpa move into an assisted living facility. The computer broke down. What sort of "communicating arsenal" can parents bring to attack these problems in a way that will keep the family functioning and healthy?

Three clear character traits that a mother and father learn from childhood include style of resolving problems, style of showing affection, and approach to traditions in the family. The sorting begins as a father and mother discuss what they see as helpful or unhealthy in the character traits they have brought to this union.

Conflict Resolution

One mother of young children was shocked and relieved when her mother-in-law toasted her husband of forty-five years at their anniversary party. The woman looked at her husband and said, "Thank you, sweetie, for the best forty-one years of my life." When everyone looked confused, she explained with a wink, "Hey, they weren't all good."

If you want to avoid conflict, you will need to go to a deserted island and live by yourself for the rest of your life. With this in mind, people must know the great challenges a couple will face in the simple to complicated problems and disagreements that are inevitable in any marriage.

Furthermore, children, especially young children, often observe the conflict from start to bitter end and see this as the way a problem should be solved. The crunched bumper of the van has fewer negative, long-term ramifications for a young child than the fight that his mother and father had later that night over the accident. Word choices and tone of voice resonate longer than the raised insurance rates.

Christ's message of forgiveness through dying on the cross for us is one that we should look to as we struggle with conflict. Extremes of conflict resolution rarely if ever offer a healthy alternative for resolving problems for a young child. A young child who witnesses parents that "blow up" over most problems, big or small, grows up blowing up at all her problems. Another child who never sees parents addressing conflict may grow up confused and unable to cope when he is involved in a confrontation.

Your children need to see that you are human. The child who observes conflict addressed and resolved understands that conflict does not have to unfold into three days of not talking to each other or aggression in words and actions. A child who observes a mother and father disagreeing and then coming to terms is a child that knows what the world is about. A child who hears you admit a mistake and apologize to another family member is a child who is sees God's gift of forgiveness in action.

Style of Affection

Your approach to affection is another character trait that affects a family. Almost all young children love to be kissed and to see others kiss. But styles of expressing affection vary widely among adults. What is commonplace and comfortable in one home might be awkward in another home.

One woman who married an especially affectionate husband explains, "Sometimes I feel awkward when he kisses me in front of the kids. I mean, I never saw my parents kissing. I just knew they loved each other. It was an unspoken sort of thing."

The husband of this same woman grew up with extremely affectionate parents. His frame of reference included love notes on the fridge and parents who openly kissed and hugged one another.

Both parents truly love each other and their children. The approach to intimacy was simply different. As with most topics, an open discussion between husband and wife about how they will show affection toward each other and their children can be helpful.

Traditions and Routine

Even a young child in a very bad home situation will embrace the tiniest tradition and routine as a comfort. Traditions and routines are predictable, safe, and often reassuring:

- praying before supper
- visiting grandparents or friends on Saturday afternoons
- placing the baby Jesus in the nativity crib on Christmas morning
- reading books together at bedtime each night
- decorating Easter eggs on Holy Saturday
- going on fun family outings on Sunday afternoons

Children find peace and comfort in tradition and routine. Parents need to establish and protect family traditions and routines.

8
Single Parents, Divorced Parents, Stepparents

"You can't prevent the birds of sorrow from flying over your head, but you can prevent them from building a nest in your hair."

CHINESE PROVERB

MANY CHILDREN TODAY are growing up in families disrupted by death, divorce, remarriage, or some other event. But different does not mean better or worse. A family with only one parent is no less a family than any other.

Nevertheless, these families experience stresses and difficulties that traditional families do not have to face. A single parent, for example, has to make all the day-to-day decisions usually shared by two parents. Often there is no one else around who can appreciate a child's unique qualities the way a parent can. Having no one with whom to share the joy of parenting can lessen the rewarding feelings that go with being a mother or father. There is no one to take turns caring for a child when the child is ill; no one with whom to discuss decisions on discipline, bedtime, friends, and privileges; no other person to answer questions, calm fears, and provide love.

Another challenge for many single parents is that they have greater financial responsibilities than parents with partners. A single mother may feel guilty about being away from her children while she works for a living, even though her married counterparts are doing the same thing.

Some single parents feel guilty about depriving their children of the other parent, so they try to compensate in various ways. Reacting to this, some children quickly learn to take advantage; they make unreasonable demands on a parent's time or ask for material things or special privileges.

Some single parents invest too much time in their children at the expense of their own well-being. They feel they shouldn't be away from their children more than is necessary, and they find it difficult to spend an evening by themselves or with friends.

Parents who are divorced are likely to find their feelings complicated by attitudes toward the ex-spouse and the past. Anger and resentment resulting from abuse, infidelity, and lack of financial support can be directed at the children—or at the other parent through the children.

Differing outlooks toward family and child-rearing are apt to become a source of friction between separated or divorced parents.

When this is the case, children may feel they are expected to take sides when, in fact, they love both parents and do not want to choose between them. Children sometimes get caught in the middle of these conflicts and react by feeling guilty or using the situation to manipulate their parents.

When there is a stepparent in the family, relationships have an added complication. Stepparents assume a certain degree of parental responsibility, but it is not the same as parenting one's own children. A stepparent, for example, may feel a need to compete with the natural parent for a child's affection. A child may feel that his "real" mother or father has been replaced by another person to whom love and loyalty are due.

Being single, divorced, or a stepparent is not only an adult circumstance; it is a family matter as well. The questions children raise about the situation need to be dealt with openly and honestly. Especially in families where divorce has occurred, children need to be reassured that they are not to blame and that their mother and father both still love them. Because they tend to see things only from an egocentric point of view, little children may feel they are somehow responsible for problems that exist between the two people they most love and depend on. If a parent remarries, children need to know that no one can replace their own mother or father and that it is all right to love and be loved by other persons.

One Parent Can Do a Good Job— With a Little Help

It is not possible for one parent to be two parents. It is possible for one parent to do a good job of parenting. But just as in two-parent situations, common sense is the norm.

Unreasonable self-sacrifice by a parent does not ensure that a child will feel loved. All parents must have realistic expectations of their ability to meet a child's needs.

One area in which single parents can use help is the development of a child's values and religious practice. In this area the relationship between a child's parents is crucial—and in a single-parent home a child does not experience this relationship. A single parent can do something about this by associating with people the child looks up to. In this way a single-parent child can witness the respect and caring that adults have for one another. Relatives, such as grandparents or aunts and uncles, can meet this need. So can friends and neighbors.

It is important for single-parent children to have contact with two-parent families because so much of childhood learning is based on experience. By observing the healthy relationships of married partners with each other and with their children, single-parent children experience other models of family life.

The Church is searching for new ways to minister to all families and to help them grow spiritually. A family with only one parent is as important as any other in the parish family. No family should feel that it does not belong in the Church community.

9
Shared Child-Raising and Day Care

"The challenge of this life is to take the stumbling blocks and make them into stepping-stones."

ANONYMOUS

THE WORLD IS constantly changing. As the world changes, we must make some changes to adjust to that world. This is not bad. This is life! The world we are in today is a much different world than twenty years ago. Some things are good. Some things are bad.

One notable change in families today is the increased number of fathers who take care of their small children. Fathers are changing diapers. They are bathing babies. They are not putting off personal involvement with their children until the children are old enough to engage in sports and other activities.

One result of such caring is closer relationships between father and child. Another result is that many fathers are discovering their nurturing side.

An even further result is that husbands and wives can communicate better with each other—because they share a greater mutual awareness of the problems and delights of nurturing. Everything about it is positive. As theologian David Thomas states, "Just as it takes both parents to create new life, we seem to appreciate more today the role of both parents in child development. As both parents communicate to the child a sense of significance, they draw from the child some of its own unique and personal gifts."

But even with the shared caring of fathers and other family members, many parents must look beyond their own families for assistance in caring for their children. More and more mothers are becoming involved in activities that take them away from their small children part of the time. Millions of preschool children are being left daily in the care of others, and it is not likely that this trend will reverse itself in the near future. Day care is one of the changes taking place in families today.

Looking at day care, we need to ask some careful questions. For example: What effect does this option have on small children and their families? How does it affect a child's development at the time? What effect is it likely to have on the child's future? How does a Christian parent retain responsibility for a child's spiritual growth when that child is cared for by someone else? If you, like many other parents, are or will be leaving your child in someone else's part-time care as you go to work, attend school, or do volunteer work, questions such as these are bound to be serious concerns.

Taking Care in Choosing Caregivers

A child-caregiver is second only to the parent in shaping a child's development. A caregiver even influences how comfortable the parent feels about her own activity away from home. So, choosing a caregiver takes time. You want someone who will carry through your influence on your child.

You may be fortunate enough to find a person who will come into your home. Most children, however, are cared for in others' homes or in day care centers. The following guidelines apply mainly to those settings.

Many parents select child care mainly because it is conveniently located or less expensive than other alternatives. That can be a mistake because some caregiving situations are not good for children. Here are three such situations:

• In some settings children are actually abused or neglected, and their basic needs for care and safety are not met. (Most caregivers are required to be licensed or registered. But even these may be meeting only minimum requirements for child care.)

• In other situations, called "custodial child care," children are not actively mistreated, but they are not sufficiently provided with stimulation to help them learn and grow.

• Finally, there are places that might provide safe care but not in a manner consistent with the parent's values in areas such as discipline and potty training.

In looking for child care, look for a situation that corresponds closely to your approach to child-rearing. The selection will usually take time. As you consider cost, location, transportation, and so on, keep in mind that you are choosing someone to represent you in caring for your child while you are absent. Your peace of mind will depend on your choice.

Look at the options. Ask lots of questions. Talk with other parents who are using the caregiver you are considering. Find out how much direct involvement you are permitted with the program. Ask questions like the following: May I drop in at any time? Will there be meetings at which we can discuss my child's needs?

Take as much time as you possibly can to choose a caregiver.

Remember, you are not relinquishing your child to someone else. Your caregiver is responsible, within reason, for carrying out your child-rearing philosophy. Your child's caregiver becomes a part of your extended family and should support your parenting role. A good child care program recognizes this responsibility, and the caregiver will develop a close relationship with the child and the family.

A good care program sees your child as a unique person, not just part of a group. Even though there may be many children to consider, the focus is on each individual child's needs which include, among other things, sleeping, eating, and playing—all of the ways a child expresses individuality.

Once you have enrolled your child in a care setting, stay involved. Monitor his or her adjustment and ongoing development. If you have concerns, share them with the caregiver. Do not presume that the caregiver knows all the answers. Don't tell yourself that you are being overprotective, that the caregiver is an expert and so she must be right, etc. Communication between you and the caregiver is really important.

Keep an open mind. Try to see the caregiver's point of view, but remain your child's advocate. That's your job.

Trust your good judgment and if your problem is not resolved, contact the government representatives who are responsible for approving child care facilities (homes or centers) in your area. Describe your concern and let them respond to it. If there is a really serious problem, it may affect children other than your own and should be dealt with.

Effects of Day Care on Children

What happens to the parent-child relationship when a child is in day care?

The social skills of children in day care vary. Different studies have reported that these children may be more independent, outgoing, cooperative, and self-confident than children who stay home. They also tend to be more boisterous than their home-reared counterparts. They are better able to make choices, and they acquire skills in dressing and grooming at an earlier age. When they start school, they generally exhibit better adjustment and more leadership abilities.

Perhaps most significantly, studies show that the parent-child relationship is not replaced or weakened by the caregiver's role, although children also form attachments with their caregivers.

A good child care setting can help your child experience loving relationships with others. It can expand the circle of security and trust which you have established with your child. But positive effects come only from good child care experiences. Carefully and wisely selected care is essential.

Some companies now offer parents the opportunity to work from home. Other companies allow "job-sharing" arrangements. This allows a parent to share a full-time position with another person. These parents are able to maintain a position in a company with benefits while still spending more time with their children. One couple was able to work out a wonderful schedule for everybody. "My husband works four longer days and watches our children on Mondays. I work Monday through Wednesday. Our children are at day care only two days a week. We all love it!"

The world is constantly changing. We can look to the world today and point to the bad things about the changes, or we can embrace each day with the different opportunities we are given. We can adjust to our world while we still embrace the Christian ideals that our parents and grandparents embraced.

10
Siblings

"Jealousy, envy and rivalry will inevitably be there. To fail to anticipate them, or to be shocked at their appearance, is an ignorance that is far from bliss."

DR. HAIM GINOTT

GOD HAS A PLAN for your family. Your role as parents in that plan is to pray for the strength to make wise decisions for your family as that plan unfolds. The journey will have many curves and bumps along the way.

Birth order, spacing, and sibling conflict are some of the many issues that parents face in raising more than one child. Once again, the problems that arise are not evidence of something awful: they are normal consequences. How you choose to address those issues is what really makes the difference in parenting several siblings.

A child's position in the family can affect his or her develop-ment. The oldest child, for example, tends to be more indepen-dent, mature, responsible, serious and anxious. This child tends to be a leader. Middle children are more likely to be spontaneous, creative, adventurous, and less stable in their moods. Youngest children are secure, affectionate, and also manipulative. They often are not willing to accept responsibility.

Children, of course, do not always match these descrip-tions—one reason being there are many other factors besides position in the family that affect personality development. These descriptions, however, do give a general picture of tendencies that can be found when a group is studied as a whole. These characteristics, moreover, last beyond childhood. In adulthood, for example, successful executives tend to be first-born children.

How can your understanding of these patterns help you and your child? It can help you to be attentive. For example, you may want to respond to your youngest child by giving the child some light responsibility within the family. You may want to give your middle child opportunities to feel special. You may want to make sure your oldest child does not worry too much or bear too much responsibility for a child.

The Spacing of Children

Another factor that can affect a child's personality develop-ment is the spacing of children in a family. For years doctors have been telling women that they should wait at least two years before another pregnancy so that their bodies will have time to recover from the previous pregnancy. On the other hand, child psychologists have found that the age between eighteen months and three years is the most difficult time for a child to accept a new baby.

Other studies indicate that children who are many years apart are less likely to have close relationships with one another when they reach adulthood.

Is there a right or wrong time to have children or a magic number of children to have? No. What is right in one situation may be inappropriate in another. Whether you have children close together or several years apart, how many children you have, whether your pregnancy "happens" or is planned, or whether you adopt children—these are all matters between you and your spouse. Ultimately, God's plan for your family will take place whether it fits in your plan or in the world's idea of what is right.

Many parents have personal reasons for the time they choose to have another child, reasons linked to their own childhood experiences with their own brothers and sisters. Other parents want to concentrate on child-rearing for a few years and then move on to further goals. Still other parents want each child to have his or her own space within the family; these parents feel that they can accomplish their goals and raise children at the same time as long as the children are not too close in age. All of these decisions are personal ones. The freedom parents have in these matters is a freedom that allows them to welcome each child as the new manifestation of God's love that he or she really is.

Preparing Children for a New Arrival

Preparing children for the birth of a new baby is important because children often react to a baby even before it is born. Children notice changes in the mother's body. Parents become preoccupied with preparation and anticipation. Friends and relatives talk about the baby and pay less attention to the child.

As a result, it is altogether natural and not at all surprising if children feel resentful and competitive.

An excellent way to involve children in the birth of the new baby is to have them help prepare the crib, fold diapers, and shop for baby clothes. Little tasks such as these help children feel that this is their baby, too.

As much as possible, children should know what is going to happen: Mother will need to go to the hospital; Grandma will come and stay; and so on. To the extent of their ability to understand, children should be given accurate information about pregnancy and childbirth. (There is more about this in the chapter on sexuality, pages 86-90.)

There is no better time to communicate about the gift of life and about our ability to share in God's creation than when it is taking place within your own family.

Jealousy

Most children have mixed feelings about a new baby. They may feel excitement, curiosity, jealousy, anger, amusement, tenderness, and warmth. All of their feelings need to be accepted. It helps your child to know that you have positive and negative feelings, too. You might say things like, "Sometimes I wish Joey wouldn't cry so much. I'm tired and need a nap. But I know he's telling me he's hungry."

If your child sees you go to soothe the baby when the baby is crying, the child may get the false impression that you have only positive feelings toward the baby. Meanwhile, the child already knows there are times when your feelings toward him or her are negative. If the child starts making this false contrast, the next step is the perception that he or she is "bad" and that the baby is "good"—or that you love the baby and not him or her.

So talk about feelings with your child—your feelings and your child's feelings. By talking about them, you show that all feelings are OK, but that you shouldn't always act on your negative feelings. For example, you may explain that you wish you could ignore the baby's crying, but you do not ignore it.

Jealousy toward a new baby is to be expected. The question is not whether the child is jealous but how strong the feeling is and how it is being expressed. Does your older child demand attention every time you pick up the baby? Is he or she whining, having toileting accidents, or showing other signs of babyish behavior? If so, these may be indications of jealousy. The baby gets attention for wet pants and crying. So the older child thinks, "These seem like good ways for me to get attention, too."

Some children have another way of coping with negative feelings. They are overly loving to the baby, as if denying the negative feelings will make them disappear.

Older children need to be reassured of their place in the family when a new baby arrives. Show each older child that he or she is special, that there is plenty of love to go around. Spend time with your older children and show an interest in their accomplishments. Involve them with the baby; don't let it appear that you and the baby have an exclusive relationship. Depending on their age, and with appropriate supervision, allow the older children to help care for and to touch the baby. Touching is important.

Point out all the things the older child is capable of doing that the baby has yet to learn. Such comparisons enhance your older child's self-image and educate the older children about the limited abilities of infants.

Sibling Conflict

As children grow older, they interact with one another in a variety of ways. Being unique individuals, they have conflicts. When such problems arise, discuss them. But don't interfere if it isn't necessary. Encourage the children to solve their problems with words. Do not allow physical fighting.

When children quarrel, they often do it to get their parent's attention. Do your best to meet each child's individual needs. Make sure they have their own "space"—both physically and emotionally. Children need an area to call their own—not necessarily a room but a place that is theirs alone and off limits to others without permission. They need to be acknowledged as individuals and to have a special relationship with each parent.

Older brothers and sisters often become models for younger children to imitate, advisors in a variety of matters, and protectors when someone needs an ally. Older siblings provide opportunities for a child to learn sharing, caring, and forgiving—opportunities that seldom come from other experiences.

Being a Catholic Family

11
Faith Development

"Just as the twig is bent, the tree's inclined."

ALEXANDER POPE

THE FAITH DEVELOPMENT of your child is part of your responsibility as a parent. Both mother and father are important in the process of religious formation. Although a mother may do more direct explanation and instruction with the child, a father's example and practice are powerful influences on the development of attitudes toward religion. In the past, the responsibility was often seen as the mother's; the father's role was not fully understood.

The importance of the relationship between mother and father in a child's faith development cannot be emphasized enough. Parents' attitudes toward one another play a major part in a child's spiritual formation.

Remember, also, that your concept of God will be shared by your child. If you say "Thank you, God, for giving me this wonderful day," you are sharing a God who gives us what is good. If you say "God doesn't like bad boys," you are sharing a judging and rejecting God. Consider the image you want your child to develop, then help form that image by your words and actions.

How Do Children Learn?

Your earliest memory of religious experience in childhood is probably of reciting prayers such as the Our Father and Hail Mary or of going to church with your family. In the past, children were involved in adult religious activities, the presumption being that they would grow to accept and understand them.

Today there is greater awareness of how children learn. However, there is still disagreement about the best ways to teach religion. Viewpoints range from "Children don't belong at Mass" to "Children need to know the Our Father even if they don't understand it."

It is true that children are not capable of understanding adult concepts and adult reasoning. But this does not mean that children should not be exposed to such concepts. They absorb what they are capable of absorbing. You do not wait until your children can cook to let them help with dinner. You start them off by having them set the table or mix a salad. Religious education works the same way. For example, a small child cannot grasp theological abstractions about God. But that does not mean you say nothing at all about God. The thing to do is to speak lovingly to your child about God. Communicate your own attitude toward God in your life.

As you teach in this way, there is no need to impose expectations or goals on your child. The child is already motivated, and the child has a model—you. So there is no need to pressure. All you need to do is permit your child to learn about religious beliefs and practices, and understanding will develop. It will happen as you join in observing the liturgical year in your home: seasons and feasts such as Advent, Christmas, Lent, Easter, and the feast of the Holy Family. These observances encourage prayer and worship as part of everyday life.

Your child can develop a sense of God through the wonder and beauty of things around him or her. The smell of a flower, the song of a bird, the colors of a rainbow can enrapture a small child. God's love surrounds you; all you need to do is point it out. These are wonderful times to say a prayer of thanksgiving with your child. Such actions help him or her internalize God's presence as it touches his or her life.

Your Own Faith Will Grow

Your child will help you grow in faith, too. You will notice things you never took time to see before, as you share the wonder of God through your child's eyes. You will find beauty and joy in your child's sharing of faith with you.

The process of using everyday experiences is important because it is difficult for a young child to think in abstract terms. The more experiential you make your child's learning, the more successful it will be. For example, you may point out, "Do you remember how special Grandma and Grandpa made you feel when we visited them? You are even more special to God than you are to Grandma and Grandpa."

Don't be concerned if your child gives God some very

human attributes such as "Does God have to take a nap?" or "Does God get colds?" Your child is apt to see God in human terms. That is good; it means that God is very real to the child. It is better to think of God this way than not at all.

As your child asks questions about God, answer them honestly and directly but simply. Too much explanation might "turn off' your son or daughter. The child will ask again if he or she wants to know more. If you don't know the answer, admit it. There are many things we as adults don't understand. If you search for answers, you and your child can learn at the same time.

If you use religious objects, select them carefully. Some religious symbols—for example, the crucified Christ, the Sacred Heart—can frighten children. If they are of poor artistic quality, they may convey an undesirable image to the child. If used only as "good luck charms," medals and statues (in cars, for example) can give false ideas about the meaning of faith.

However, well-chosen religious objects can be used to expand a child's understanding. A child will develop a sense of reverence, for instance, in a home where a well-chosen statue or picture is in a special area for prayerful quiet and reflection. It is important to stress that these objects are symbols: they represent and point to something else.

Are you wondering how to explain God as Father, Son, and Spirit to your child? This concept is difficult enough for adults; there is no way it can be grasped by a child. Some religious educators suggest teaching children only about God the Father. Other educators disagree, saying that many children cannot relate to God as a good father because those children's experience of their male parent is far from ideal. Leaving that question aside, all can agree that children have positive experiences of Christmas and Easter. From these experiences children can be led to appreciate the true meaning of these feasts if they are made aware that these are celebrations of Jesus' birth and Resurrection.

As you share the story of Christmas, you will also be teaching your child about Mary and other members of Jesus' human family.

There are many excellent books available to parents that deal with religion and faith development in the early years. A few of these books are listed on page 111.

Faith development is a lifelong process for you as well as for your child. Too often we expect the religious education we acquired as children to last a lifetime. Part of our responsibility as Christians is to keep nourishing our faith through prayer, the sacraments, reading, other forms of adult education, and participation in the Church community.

When you nourish your faith in these ways, you and your child can journey together toward God and a fuller understanding of Jesus' word. The beauty of the children God gives us is that he renews our own faith through them.

12
Prayer in the Family

"Young or old, we learn to pray by praying. We come to be at home with prayer. And home is what and where prayer must be. If prayer is to be familiar ground, a place where we are comfortable, then prayer needs to flow through life where it is lived."

GABE HUCK

YOUR CHILD'S DEVELOPING AWARENESS of God's presence in your home and family includes a need to speak with God. As the child's image of God is formed through the experiences of everyday life, ways of communicating with him also need to be encouraged.

Prayer is our primary means of communing with God. A family that fully expresses its role as domestic Church will find prayer a necessary part of its life. This does not mean that a great deal of time must be spent in prayer. It simply means that the family makes prayer a regular part of its life instead of praying only when there is enough time or when there is a crisis. What matters is that you and your child accept prayer as a basic part of your lives.

Example Is an Effective Teacher

Your example is the most effective teacher your child can have. If prayer is important to you, it will be important to your child.

Not only when you pray but how you pray forms a significant impression. Do you kneel and pray the rosary in the privacy of your bedroom? Do you joyfully exclaim "God, thank you for this beautiful spring morning"? Do you pause for quiet moments of reflection as you go about your duties? These are all examples of prayer.

The content of your prayer also affects your child's own development of prayer life. Are your prayers those of praise and thanksgiving? Do you pray for guidance, for forgiveness, for favors? Why is prayer important to you?

Prayer is part of your personal relationship with God. In this regard, remember: your image of God affects your relationship with God and the way you express this relationship in prayer. When you pray together, you strongly influence your child's image of God and relationship with him.

Prayer is also important to your participation in a community of Christians. You need to experience prayer by yourself. You also need to experience it with others—as husband and wife together, as parent and child together, within the entire family, within the community. And just as you need to experience prayer both in personal and in community settings, your child needs this too. As soon as he is able to speak to God in his own words, encourage him to do it. And involve him in family prayer as well.

Making time for family prayer can be difficult in today's busy household. The best time will not be the same in every home. The best times are the ones that work for you, whether they be during the evening meal, at bedtime, early in the morning, or at midday.

Formal Prayer or Spontaneous Prayer?

Should little children be expected to learn the Our Father, or is it better for them to speak to God in their own words? There is really no need to make such a choice. There is room both for spontaneous and for formal prayer.

Although a three-year-old cannot possibly appreciate the beauty and significance of the Lord's Prayer, the prayer was given to us by Jesus himself and is a vital part of our Christian heritage. It can be truly inspiring to anyone, including a child, to witness a community of Christians praying the Lord's Prayer together. Children can sense great meaning from this experience, even if they do not understand all of the words.

Little children should be exposed to formal prayers, but they should not be forced to memorize them. Rather, they should be encouraged to speak with God in their own language, at their own level of ability, as if conversing with a good friend or a parent. After all, their relationship with

God is modeled on relationships experienced with the people in their lives.

The early prayers of your child will be very concrete. Grace at meals may call on God to bless each fork, napkin, and dish of food on the table. Bedtime may bring a request for God to provide a new toy or to make a big sister stop teasing. To your younger child, these are the important things.

Spontaneous, informal prayer also is important. It is not something for children to do only until they are old enough to understand more mature language. Many adults do not feel comfortable expressing their faith through spontaneous prayer. But expressing your thoughts and feelings in your own words is just as important to you as it is to your child. Remember, the words of Jesus in the Our Father were originally his spontaneous prayer. When you communicate with God in your own words, you let your child know that it is acceptable for adults as well as children.

You may wonder about the rosary or other devotional forms. Praying in these ways by yourself is a wonderful example to your child because the child sees that these devotions are meaningful to you. However, little children are not able to remain attentive for very long. So, in the family setting, short prayers, songs, and meditations may be more appropriate.

If you need guidance in developing family prayer times, see the resources listed on page 111.

Mary and the Bible

You may have grown up feeling a special closeness to Mary, the spiritual mother of all Christians. She was a special example of openness to God's will. As Jesus' mother, she shared many of the experiences of all parents, even though her child was the Son of God. If you communicate to your child your devotion to Mary, you give your child the opportunity to develop similar feelings.

The use of Scripture with young children is sometimes a concern to parents. Bible stories should be chosen carefully for the message they contain. Many lessons of Scripture cannot be grasped by small children. You may wish to tell the story to the child in your own words so that you communicate the message you want your child to hear.

The important thing is not so much how, where, or when you pray. The important thing is that prayer flows through your life.

13
Education
in the Family

Ian's mother turned to him at the lunch table and asked, "What did you learn in Sunday school today, Ian?"

Three year-old Ian replied, "Oh, we learned about Jesus and his fossils, but not the type I know you are thinking of, Mom. These fossils were the guys he hung out with, not dinosaurs."

THE ULTIMATE EDUCATION for a child's faith begins at home. This is the one of the strongest messages this book hopes to instill in the readers. Parents model faith in a simple gesture of blessing a child before he goes to sleep and in the amazing effort it takes to get everyone to church on time—especially when sleeping in is a real temptation.

Parents have the main role in teaching a child about faith in the Catholic family, but the greatest supplement is the school or parish that teaches Catholic education to the child. Eventually the child will experience the sacraments of Eucharist, Reconciliation, and Confirmation in the schools or programs which the parents have chosen for that child. Parents of young children have so much to look forward to.

This partnership is one that even the youngest child observes as the parents take interest in what he or she learned in Sunday school. Signing children up for Bible Camp and singing the songs they learned with them encourages a positive spirit in learning about God. Sunday School, Bible Camp—so many great opportunities exist for a young child to engage in even before he or she goes to school.

One mother of an eighth-grade son commented, "Experiencing the sacraments through my son has been a wonderful thing for me. I feel that the programs are much better today than when I was growing up. I remember memorizing prayers and not really understanding what was really going on. My son has service hours and events surrounding Confirmation that are so neat. I feel that he is living the sacrament. The teachers are asking much more of the parents today too."

It is never too early to start thinking about the future choice of educational partnership for your son or daughter. The parent of a young child should consider the avenue that bests suits his or her family. Does a Catholic school fit into the financial budget? Will your child need special assistance from a public school? Does a CCD program work better for your children? This decision should be one upon which both parents agree.

Finally, parental involvement in the community is an education in and of itself! The young child who sees his mother or father volunteering at parish functions and participating in the liturgy as an usher or a Eucharistic Minister is learning about community.

14
Celebration in the Christian Family

The way each family celebrates is unique, and these celebrations become traditions which, handed down from generation to generation, develop into warm and wonderful occasions to say thank you to God for the "specialness" of that family.

TIMES OF CELEBRATION in Christian families are a gift you give one another. You are communicating the value of family to your child. You are giving a sense of belonging to your child and affirming his or her identity. You are sharing the love you have for one another, a love generated from God and given to you by God. You are making memories for them to cherish later in life.

The opportunities for celebration in your family are unlimited, as are the ways in which you celebrate. Events are important to a child when they involve things a child can touch and experience. For example, a prayer service celebrating the arrival of a new puppy means much more to a four-year-old child than elaborate rituals commemorating Labor Day. Many religious bookstores carry a variety of books to celebrate these exciting moments that add depth and closeness to family life.

Liturgy and Family Traditions

For many children the sacraments provide a chance to celebrate with grandparents, aunts, uncles, cousins, etc. Whether it is a baptism, marriage, first Communion, or another sacrament, participation in both the ceremony and the accompanying activities is special to your children, particularly when the event is shared by others who are important to them. Take advantage of the family activities designed to enrich these experiences. Although children may not fully understand the spiritual significance of the occasion, they appreciate the love and joy and become aware that these are meaningful and special times in the lives of Catholic families.

Family traditions are a wonderful legacy that give children a sense of belonging and strengthen their feeling of family identity.

Establishing New Family Traditions

Besides preserving traditions that are inherited from earlier generations, your family can establish new traditions. Rituals can become eagerly anticipated moments in your family history.

Children particularly enjoy hearing the story of their own birth and other events special to them and their family. The day they were born, arrived at home, were baptized, etc., can be recounted with joy over and over. Pictures and other mementos can be shared, renewing memories of special times.

Some families celebrate each child's baptismal day. On his or her day, the child's baby and baptismal pictures, newspaper announcement, cards or gifts are displayed in a prominent place. The child chooses the dinner menu or a family fun activity for celebration—whatever reinforces the idea that he or she is a special child of God, loved and called by name in baptism.

It is important to help your child feel part of the family celebration. One way you can do this is by show-and-tell: encourage your child to draw a picture and then talk about it, telling you what the event means to him or her. Let the child say a prayer, hold a candle, or carry a flower. Relate what is happening in terms of the child's past experiences. Explain in advance what will be happening, then give her or him a chance to ask questions.

You can also make reaching out to others a part of the celebration. It could take the form of sharing with an elderly person who is alone, or with a special friend. It might take the form of encouraging your child to share gifts with others. A basket of food might be given to a needy family, with the child helping to select the items. The child might make gifts for someone in a nursing home. A child's companionship, all by itself, can be a gift to a lonely person.

Cherish your times of celebration as joyous occasions when you affirm God's love, and your love for one another. Celebrate!

15
Celebration of the Mass
With Your Child

"Our weekly liturgy is called Eucharist, a word that means thanksgiving. The actions we do there, the blessing and sharing of bread and wine, is a gathering of what our lives have been and the strength for new living. The giving of thanks that happens over the gifts of bread and wine is the very shape of our Christian life."

GABE HUCK

THE EUCHARISTIC LITURGY is, in the words of the Second Vatican Council, "the fount and apex of the whole Christian life." Nevertheless, the liturgy of the Mass is usually planned for adult participants, and there is no way a small child can fully understand its meaning.

This raises a practical question: Should you take your child to Mass or not? You may feel that it is better to leave your child in someone else's care. Or you may enroll him or her in a preschool class that meets during Mass. Or you and your spouse may take turns going to church while one of you stays home with your child. These alternatives are worth considering; each option has its pros and cons. If you and your spouse go to Mass at separate times, you miss an opportunity to worship together, to share your sacrament of marriage with the community. If you leave your child with someone else, he may feel left out of something he senses is a special time for you, and he may resent your going to church without him.

Ways to Make Church an Experience of Love

If you include your child in the Eucharistic celebration, make it as meaningful an expression as possible. If Mass is an unpleasant experience for a small child, it can be harmful to the child's developing attitudes toward religion.

The most important thing your child can experience in church is love. We come together in Eucharist to celebrate God's love for us. Your child learns about God's love through your love, which she sees and feels. This love, ever present, should be communicated very clearly in church, God's place.

To many small children the experience of going to church means reminders to sit still, threats of punishment, scowls and angry looks—sometimes even shakes, pokes, and slaps. It should be no surprise that children who endure such experiences do not look forward to going to church.

This does not mean that children must be allowed to do as they please in church, distracting their parents, the celebrant, and others in the worship community. Children need to learn to behave appropriately at Mass, but there are loving and gentle ways to do this. There are ways to make going to church a meaningful experience that your child will look forward to. Here are a few suggestions.

• First of all, do not expect adult behavior from your child. Activities such as kneeling for long periods, or listening to the homily from beginning to end, are unreasonable expectations of a small child. Try to put yourself in your child's place. A child may not be able to see over the top of the pew when kneeling, or see anything but people's backs unless you hold the child or sit close to the altar. A child may be afraid to stay in the pew alone at communion time.

• Use positive kinds of interaction to help your child act appropriately. Let Christ's love flow. For example, give a hug instead of a swat if your child is restless. Cuddle him on your lap as you listen to the homily. Touch your lips or remind him to whisper instead of saying "Be quiet!" Your gentle touch can calm more surely than a threat.

• At special times say "I need to listen to Father's words" or "I want to talk to God." Teach with love rather than fear.

• Choose appropriate distractions. Call his attention to a statue, a banner, etc. Let him bring a book or a stuffed animal with him. Paraphrase the gospel or a prayer. Explain the message of the homily.

• Call attention to highlights of the Mass. Have your child watch for the presentation of the gifts or listen for the bells at the Gloria or other festive moments. Encourage the child to sing the "Amen" or "Alleluia." Share the sign of peace and help your child do the same with others.

Some communities today hold a children's liturgy during which young children leave the families during the Liturgy of the Word. Lay ministers will read the gospel and speak to the children on their level regarding the message of the gospel. Other communities encourage the children to bring the family's offertory envelope up to the altar during the time of offertory collection. All of these measures positively include children in the Mass.

• Make sure you let your child know what you like about his or her behavior in church. Words such as "You tried really hard to be quiet" or "I'm glad you sang Holy, Holy" are better than "You were good" (or "You were bad").

You may feel you are giving up an important part of your own worship experience when you take time to make the Mass meaningful to your child. But teaching your child about God is part of your vocation as a parent. God has called you to be a mother or father. For a few years at least, your uninterrupted participation in the Eucharistic celebration may be as difficult to achieve as windows without fingerprints on them!

Remember, too, that liturgy is community prayer, not private prayer, and that your child is part of that community. When you are reaching out in love to someone else as part of celebration your prayer may take a different form, but it is not diminished.

There may be times when your child will not respond to your best efforts. Then you must let him know that he has no right to disrupt the worship of others. If his behavior goes beyond acceptable limits and positive alternatives fail, you may need to get up and leave or discipline your child. Alternatives such as these are discussed in the chapter on discipline on pages 80-86. The focus here is on positive methods to help your child value going to church. If it is a loving experience, your child will want to do whatever is necessary to be included.

16
Inter-Church and Interfaith Families

Robin told her friend Julie,
"My dad isn't Catholic, but my mom loves him anyway."

MANY PEOPLE TODAY are married to persons of different faiths. The success of these marriages, as well as the religious development of the children in these families, depends on how husbands and wives respond to their faith differences.

Faith differences can occur even in marriages where both partners belong to the same faith tradition. Some Catholics, for example, are more active in practicing their faith than others. One spouse may go to daily Mass, the other occasionally on Sunday. The ways in which they express their spiritual commitment may not agree; one spouse may prefer a traditional approach while the other has a liberal approach to Church practice and teaching.

Issues such as these can cause tension and conflict in a marriage, making the children's faith development a difficult matter. But there are also similarities: feelings and viewpoints that spouses share in common.

Regardless of your differences, there will be similarities in your beliefs. Identify these similarities and stress them with your spouse and with your child. Then your family prayer and celebrations can reflect these shared faith values. If you identify the aspects of faith that you have in common and reflect these shared faith values, your child will come to know God through your love.

Good communication between husband and wife is particularly necessary in interfaith families. Make every effort to listen to your partner's views and feelings and to share your own. Understanding is not the same as agreeing, but resolving differences starts with understanding what the differences are.

Make sure you understand what you believe and are able to explain it. In this regard, do not presume that ideas you learned as a child are still adequate for you as an adult. Adults need adult understanding of their faith. A great help in recent years are adult religious education programs. Many dioceses and parishes offer interesting mini-courses in Scripture, theology, and so on. By taking advantage of such opportunities, you may discover that you and your spouse are not so far apart in what you believe. Perhaps you differ mainly in how you express or practice your faith.

Above all, take great care to respect one another's point of view. It does not help to prove each other wrong or to force your spouse to accept your beliefs. This can lead only to resentment or rejection. Love and sharing are based on mutual respect and acceptance of each other as you are.

Sharing Responsibility

Both parents need to support the child's spiritual development. This is not only Dad's duty or Mom's job. In the early years, the content of your child's faith development is so general that there is hardly a possibility of faith differences becoming an issue. As the child grows up, this situation could change—in which case neither parent should be expected to compromise his or her faith convictions. But at the early stage, the essential element in faith development is your child's coming to know God through your love—a responsibility you both share fully.

Above all, do not try to get your child to take sides if you and your spouse have conflicts about religion. That is unfair; a small child cannot possibly understand the principles involved. In a situation like that, a child feels forced to choose sides. As a result the God you want your child to know through the experience of love becomes an actual threat to love.

Raising Children in Today's World

17
Self-Esteem

"The type of love most important for the normal personality development of the child is the kind that says, 'I love you...not for what you do or don't do, but just because you're you.'"

WILLIAM E. HOMAN, M.D.

THREE-YEAR-OLD SARAH asked her mother. "Do you like me?"

"Yes, I do," her mother replied.

"Does Daddy like me?" Sarah persisted.

Her mother answered that he did.

"Sue and Joan like me, too?" Sarah then asked.

Her mother's reply was that, yes, her sisters liked her, too.

With a sigh of contentment, Sarah summarized: "Everybody likes me!"

All children need to feel good about themselves. The knowledge that they are valued and important is absolutely necessary to their healthy development. No matter how capable or knowledgeable they become, this belief in their own worth is essential to their well-being and overall adjustment in life. They can accept God's love and the love of others only if they feel worthy of love.

Your child's basic attitude toward herself as a person worthy of love and respect is well established by age four or five. Your acceptance of this child just as she is, acceptance with no strings attached, your support of the child's attempts at competence—these are ways in which you demonstrate in human terms the unconditional love God has for each of us.

A healthy self-concept, or self-esteem, begins in infancy. Your unconditional love for your baby, your willingness to meet his or her needs, says that he or she is someone very unique and special. Your son or daughter is valued not for what he or she does but for who the child is. This acceptance for simply "being" is fundamental to a positive self-concept.

As your child grows older, the positive messages you have already given are expanded. Smiles and hugs given unconditionally tell the child that she is worthy of love. When you offer to read her a story you are saying she is worthy of your time. As you interrupt your work to admire a bug your son found outdoors, you are letting him know that his enthusiasm is important to you.

On a side note, parents should always consider the danger that lies in telling children that they are better than others or that they are good when they misbehave. Many parents confuse the concept of a "healthy" self-esteem with a "high" self-esteem. Family psychologist John Rosemond says that Hitler had a high self-esteem, implying that those who believe that they are better than others develop an elitist attitude.

In addition, those young children who are told that everything they do is great, even in situations when they may have been wrong, become confused. Guiding your child to find a healthy self-concept—not one with feelings of low self-worth or one with extreme feelings of entitlement—is a difficult yet important challenge. In the end, a child should know that he or she will be aware of people who are gifted in certain areas and people who are not as gifted in certain areas as they are. A "healthy" child knows this and is still happy in the knowledge that God loves him or her.

Decision-Making and Positive Reinforcement

Give your child the opportunity to express his or her unique personality. Begin early to encourage the child to make decisions. Give choices whenever possible. At first, these choices may entail little things, such as whether to wear a red shirt or a blue one. Allowing such choices tells your child that he or she is capable of making decisions and that you have enough respect to let him or her do so. Such opportunities build a positive self-concept and the child's awareness of personal uniqueness.

Feelings Are Not Bad, They're Just Feelings

Accept your child's feelings. Children—and adults—have little control over how they feel. What they do about their feelings is another matter. Your child's feelings are such an important part of his or her self-concept that if you reject, punish, or fail to acknowledge those feelings, you are seriously affecting the child's self-esteem.

Little children often experience feelings of anger, fear, and jealousy. These feelings are not "bad" because feelings are neither good nor bad. They just are.

Encourage your child to share feelings with you. You may need to put the feelings into words at first—for example, "I think you are angry because you can't play outside." Eventually, your child will say it himself, "I'm angry because I can't play outside." You can then say, "I know having to play inside makes you angry. Why don't you do your new puzzle now, and maybe it will be warmer this afternoon?" Don't say, "That's nothing to be upset about." If you say that, you are telling your child that his feeling is not important. Acknowledge and accept the feeling as valid, because it is.

Feelings are one thing. Behavior is another. Behavior based on feelings may not be acceptable, and you do not need to permit it. You may need to say, "I know you are jealous because Mom and I are going out tonight, but you may not throw your toys at me."

Here you are accepting the feeling but not the behavior. (This will be discussed in greater detail in Chapter 19 on Discipline. At this point, remember that your role is to help your child find appropriate ways to express feelings and to deal with them.) Acceptance of feelings is an important part of the growth of self-esteem.

Give in—Once in a While

When you and your child disagree, it is all right for you to give in once in a while. This, too, is important to the child's self-concept. Occasionally doing things the child's way does not mean that you are rearing a selfish child. Rather, this tells the child that his or her views are also important and that you think enough of him or her to give up your own preference. For example, if you want to have chicken for dinner and your son asks for hamburgers, save the chicken for another time. If your daughter prefers the pink dress to the blue, buy the one she likes.

This in no way means that your child must always come first. It does not mean that you must sacrifice yourself and always be available to support your child's interests. If you did that, you might come to resent the intrusion and react with hostility. And your child might fail to realize that you yourself need to be valued and affirmed for more than just what you do for him.

Another thing to watch for is the tendency to use your child to build your own self-esteem. That can be dangerous. What your child needs is to develop his or her own potential, not to "turn out" the way you want. You can, of course, feel joy in being a parent and take pride in your child's accomplishments But let the emphasis remain on sharing his or her development. This satisfaction is an important part of parenting.

Admit Mistakes and
Play Down Competition

Being able to admit your mistakes is part of a healthy self-concept, for you as well as for your child. If you were wrong, say so. For example, if you punished your child for knocking over a plant and then you find out the dog did it, say you made a mistake and apologize. Doing this tells your child that you value him or her enough to seek forgiveness and that you care about his or her feelings. It also lets your son or daughter know that nobody needs to pretend to be perfect. Your child will then be more likely to acknowledge his or her own mistakes when they occur.

Finally, as much as possible, play down the element of competition in your child's achievements During the early years it is far more important for a child to learn to feel confident of his or her abilities than to be better than someone else. If there is a winner there has to be a loser, and losing is damaging to self-esteem. Ours is a highly competitive society. Competition is built into work, recreation social status, education, etc. Achieving is important, but people do not tend to judge themselves on their own merits; they tend only to see how they compare with others.

Give your child the kind of love that builds self-confidence during his or her formative years. If you do that, your child will have the self-esteem so necessary for happiness and success in the years to come.

18
Moral Development

Children do not have the ability to understand mature morality, but your consistency in guidance and the children's knowledge that morality is important to you will help them develop Christian values.

YOU WILL WANT TO GIVE your son or daughter the training necessary to make appropriate moral decisions in adulthood. For example, you will want your child to realize that stealing, cheating, and lying are wrong. In early childhood a child does not have the ability to understand such things and to make decisions about them based on fully developed moral reasoning. This ability is just emerging in the child.

As in all other areas of personal development, your own example of morality is of greatest importance. The knowledge that you take moral issues seriously will influence your child's attitudes. As a parent, you should understand the various stages of moral development and your own important role in it.

Six Stages of Moral Development

Psychologist Lawrence Kohlberg has defined six stages of moral development. When an individual progresses through these stages, he or she goes through them in a definite order. No stage can be skipped, nor can the stages be reversed.

Development from Stage One to Stage Six, however, is not automatic. Not all persons reach a mature level of moral functioning. Some adults simply do not reach a stage where they are capable of making mature moral decisions. The kind of thinking that goes into moral decision-making at the highest level does not even make sense to these people.

Furthermore, people who do have the capability of mature moral reasoning do not always use that capability. For example, a teenager who steals a car may have a thorough understanding of the laws against theft. But his understanding does not keep him from placing his own pleasure ahead of the rules of society.

To an infant, "good" means whatever satisfies a need. Unaware of the needs of others, the child is concerned only with his own wants. This is consistent with his overall development. What satisfies him is good; anything that delays gratification is bad.

Stage One

In the first stage of development, moral judgment is closely tied to the satisfaction of wants. The same act may be seen as good or bad. If the person is caught or punished, for example, the act is "bad." Eating candy before dinner is all right if Mom doesn't find out; it's wrong if she catches you and you are punished. The person at this first level has some awareness of authority, but, basically, the person judges the goodness or badness of the act by its consequences.

Stage Two

In the second stage the individual gradually reaches a point where behavior is determined more by positive consequences than by negative ones. The child reasons, "If I help Mom with the dishes, maybe I'll get to go to a movie." At this point the person understands morality thus: Doing what those in authority want is good because it gets rewards. The motivation becomes focused more on pursuit of pleasure than avoidance of punishment, but it is still primarily generated by self-gain.

Stage Three

At the third stage of moral development, some general standards of behavior are set. There is now an awareness of, and concern for, doing what is right. However, the reason for appropriate behavior is focused more on being accepted and approved of than on the action itself. There is concern with belonging, being liked. Helping to prepare dinner is valued because it earns approval, not because of a sense of responsibility to the family.

Stage Four

When an individual reaches the fourth stage, rules and regulations become the absolute criteria for behavior. This is often referred to as "law and order" morality. Rules are not violated. The laws have been established for the benefit of society and must be followed totally in everyone's best interest. The individual does not question whether the rule is just.

Stages Five and Six

The last two stages of moral development are those which go beyond external controls. Here, the mature individual makes moral decisions based on principles he or she has internalized. Laws remain important because the person understands the need for them, not just because they exist. Decisions are based on convictions of one's own conscience. Political dissidents are an example of this level. In countries that restrict freedom of speech, dissidents often risk punishment by speaking out.

They are led by deep convictions which take precedence over established rules.

As mentioned before, not all adults reach the highest levels of moral reasoning. Some, for example, base their moral decisions on hoped-for rewards or fear of punishment (Stage One or Two). Many adults follow rules simply because they exist (Stage Four). Adolescents tend to be very concerned with approval and acceptance by others (Stage Three).

Young Children and Moral Development

Young children do things primarily to satisfy their own wishes. Their ability to put themselves in someone else's place is quite limited. They are unable to understand that laws apply to everyone, at all times, in every situation.

To a small child's moral reasoning, something is OK if Mom or Dad doesn't find out about it. Getting caught is what is to be avoided, not the action itself.

The ability to judge the act rather than the consequences comes much later, when rules are seen as being ever-present and unchanging or when the sense of justice becomes internalized rather than imposed by society.

This does not mean that you must wait until your child is older to expect appropriate behavior or that you should not try to explain your reasons for wanting him to act in a certain way. The more practice your child has in making moral decisions, with your guidance, the more ready he or she will be to advance in moral reasoning.

What You Can Do

There are things you can do to help your child develop moral judgment. Here are some suggestions:

In the early years, make certain that there are consistent consequences for behavior. When behavior is appropriate, reward it. When behavior is unacceptable, have consequences such as loss of a privilege or a scolding. Be consistent: Don't punish your child for jumping on a chair one day, ignore it the next day, and laugh at his childish antics the third day. Always follow behavior with a consequence that says, this is acceptable or not acceptable. Also, consequences should take into account the severity of the child's misbehavior.

Encourage your child to make decisions about the way he or she or someone else should act. You can use stories for this purpose. For example, ask "Why do you think the little girl got hurt?" or "What if she did such and such?" This will give you an opportunity to understand your child's moral reasoning, and it will provide him or her with an opportunity to solve a moral problem. Have the child consider alternatives, being careful not to give your solution as the "right" one. This is a time to stretch your son's or daughter's awareness, not to prove a point. Your child's reasoning is just as right for him or her as yours is for you.

Help your child to consider options in real-life situations. If your child has money he can spend either to buy his father a birthday present or to get something for himself, what are his options? What will the results be? Help your child to consider alternatives. You may want to let the child decide, or you may want to tell your child to buy the gift. Whichever option you choose, encourage some discussion first. Opportunities to resolve questions of this kind are valuable for your child.

What role does religion play in moral development? Religious beliefs and values are a guide to moral judgment. Religion and morality are not the same thing. On the one hand, many adults who sincerely practice their faith are immature in their moral development. Some people who know and believe in the Ten Commandments have abortions, cheat on their income tax, and are unfaithful to their spouses without considering these things wrong. On the other hand, some people who profess no religious affiliation have deeply ingrained moral and ethical principles.

Religion helps people to be more aware of their moral options. It offers guidance in decision-making much as you help your child make choices by discussing the alternatives. All by itself, however, religion will not provide moral maturity.

Like religion, the concept of sin is related to moral judgment but is separate from it. A small child is not capable of understanding the full impact of his actions. His sense of responsibility to God and to others is just developing. He lacks the full awareness of the significance of his acts that is necessary for serious sin to occur.

There is disagreement as to whether or not young children are capable of sin. Certainly there are times when a child deliberately ignores a parent's direction or willfully hurts a friend. Acts such as these can and should be of concern. But there should be greater concern for patterns of behavior that may be signs of serious personal problems. This is why the need for consistent consequences on the part of parents is so needed: to prevent these potentially serious patterns from developing.

More than consequences, however, children need to know that they are surrounded by others in whose love they can trust. The focus should always be on positive aspects of behavior so that motivation comes from the knowledge that "I am good." Then, even when mistakes are made, the search for goodness in self and others provides an incentive to try again to do better.

Finally, your own example is of greatest importance to your child. Your own moral judgment is a powerful model. Let your child know that you, too, struggle with moral questions. Share the kind of answers you want your child to find someday. Although your small child probably will not understand your reasoning, the knowledge that you take moral issues seriously will be a strong influence. Remember, because God made this interesting yet complicated world for us, we can always pray to him for guidance in dealing with the moral issues that go along with it.

19
Discipline

"Knowledge about child development can help us become more self-confident, flexible, resilient and resourceful, but it cannot produce perfect children.... Every normal, healthy child is upsetting, unlovable and difficult at times."

EDA J. LESHAN

YOUR UNCONDITIONAL LOVE for your child is the most important part of your role as a parent. Love is necessary for the development of a positive self-concept and is the basis of your child's image of God. Your love and acceptance of your child as a unique and special gift of God must be present in every part of the parent-child relationship.

How does discipline fit into this picture? Does unconditional love for your child mean you must allow the child to dictate the terms of your relationship?

Of course not. God loves us without reservation, but does not condone everything we do. As a loving parent, you must make discipline a part of your relationship with your child. You cannot rear your child to healthy, mature adulthood without providing discipline. The discipline is rooted in your love, which has its origins in the love of God. It shows that you love and care about Him.

Young children need boundaries. In particular, they need the security of boundaries imposed on them from outside themselves. Discipline gives your child the limits necessary for developing trust in the world in which he or she is growing up.

Punishment, Discipline, and Self-Discipline

Punishment is one form of discipline. But discipline includes all the things you do to help your child learn to behave the way you want. You use discipline so that your child will do what is right. If you think of discipline as taking place whenever you interact with your child, you will not need to depend as much on punishment. The best form of discipline sets the stage for appropriate behavior to take place.

Discipline should be phrased as positively as possible. The behavior, rather than the person, should be the focus. Telling your child "People feel sad when you call them names" describes behavior, whereas "You're a mean kid!" labels a person. Saying "I'll wait until you pick up your toys and then we'll have lunch" is more positive than "You're not getting any lunch until you pick up your toys." Telling a crying child, "I told you it's too cold to play outside. Now find something to do," sends a different message than "I know you want to play outside, but it's too cold. Why don't we get your blocks out of the closet?"

The goal in disciplining children should be to help them in becoming self-disciplining. Ask yourself, "How can my child best learn from this situation?" Identify what you want your child to learn, then provide the learning experience in a growth-producing manner that does not threaten his or her self-esteem.

Some adults assume that little children are not "old enough to understand." As a result, these adults do not use talking to children as a means of discipline. Yet, even infants learn the meaning of no and hot very quickly.

Many children do not understand cause-effect relationships. But when someone describes the possible results of their action, they are not likely to repeat it. A four-year-old, for example, is capable of understanding why looking carefully before crossing the street is essential. The explanation for doing this might not be the same explanation given to an adult, but the result will be the same. Talking to children, letting them know "This is important," will oftentimes help them to remember to act appropriately, just from their desire to please you.

Children are egocentric. This does not mean they are self-centered in a negative sense. It means that a child's point of view is limited to his or her perspective. For example, Bobby knows he wants this toy, but he cannot comprehend that Sandy wants it or has a right to it just as much as he does. So, you need to explain, "Sandy wants to play with it too. She likes the truck as much as you do."

Many Effective Ways to Discipline

Helping your child to understand the difference between feelings and actions is important to effective discipline. For example, it is OK for a person to feel angry; it is not OK to hurt the person with whom we are angry. Often children can deal with angry feelings if they are encouraged to describe them. Words are powerful, and children can use words rather than resorting to physical means. Saying "Stop it," "That's mine," "You hurt my feelings" are effective words a child can learn as an alternative to fighting.

It may also be helpful to role-play with your child, acting out alternative and more effective ways to handle situations. Children, for example, sometimes say "No one wants to play with me" when they have not even approached anyone or have done so in a negative manner. You might say "I think you want to be friends with Tim and Don, but they get angry when you call them names. Why don't you say 'Can I play with you?'" Your modeling the appropriate behavior in this way gives your child an opportunity to acquire the skill of entering a play group.

Another technique that is often effective with very young children is that of diversion. For example, if your child is about to grab a fragile object on Aunt Sue's end table, a tactic that often works is to divert his attention to a favorite toy, thus saving the precious object. This tactic also works to some extent with older preschoolers, but don't rely on it as frequently as with infants. Three- and four-year-olds can understand simple explanations, limits, and consistent rules. They also are less willing to accept diversion.

Another learning experience might be restitution in which even small children can participate. For example, if a child makes crayon marks on walls, have him or her help scrub them off. (Assist only if necessary, and make sure the work is not much fun.)

Sometimes children learn if you let natural or logical consequences take place. For example, if you have reminded your son that the dog will eat his snack if it is left on the floor, and he continues to leave it there, let the dog eat the snack.

Separation from activity, or from an area or an individual, is another means of intervention that can be used. Telling your child "You will have to play inside because you threw sand at the other children" might be an appropriate disciplinary procedure.

"Time Out" is a form of separation, but it is more restrictive and often more punishing. Here the child usually is isolated (on a chair, in his room) and not permitted to pursue other activities. Saying "You must sit here until you are ready to pick up the crayons you threw on the floor" is an example of Time Out. With older children, a statement such as "Hitting is against the rules. I want you to sit here for three minutes and think of some other ways to let Megan know you are angry. Then we'll talk about it" may be an appropriate use of Time Out.

On rare occasions restraint of a child may be necessary to prevent injury to herself or others, damage to property, or to ensure compliance with rules. To a child who has lost control of her emotions it may be reassuring to have someone hold her so that she does not hurt herself or others. Restraint should be done as calmly and gently as possible. It should not be undertaken by an adult who is angry or otherwise upset.

A child who repeatedly attacks another child may need to be restrained by an adult until she is calm enough to discuss the problem or to find another activity. A child who insists on hitting her brother may need to be told, "I will hold you until you are ready to talk to Jeff about your feelings."

As often as possible, a situation in which discipline is necessary should be structured so that a change in the child's behavior ends the need for the disciplinary action to continue (for example, "When you are calm…" "When you are ready to pick up the crayons…"). This linking of discipline to the child's behavior is an important element in the learning of self-discipline.

Spanking Is Not Effective Punishment

Punishment in the form of spanking is rarely the best method of discipline for parents to use. It usually indicates a loss of emotional control by the adult rather than a serious offense by the child. It meets the need of the adult to vent feelings of anger and frustration. It does not teach the child acceptable behavior. It does not preserve self-esteem. It is not growth-producing. Spanking should never be the method of choice for discipline of young children by their parents or others. Generally, the more spanking is used, the less effective it becomes. If you do resort to spanking your child, use it only in really serious situations where other methods have failed. And always look for better means of discipline.

Sometimes parents lose control and hurt their children. If you have difficulty controlling your temper, or your child's behavior is really upsetting you, you should talk to somebody to help you deal with your problem. This does not mean that you are a bad parent or that you do not love your child. What it means is that you need some support in dealing with your child's behavior or in taking care of yourself. Your local social service agency or parish can help you find someone to give this support.

Firmness and consistency are key ingredients in discipline. If you discipline your child, you should follow through—unless you were wrong to begin with. Discipline should be consistent and not depend on factors such as the mood you are in or how busy you happen to be. Children become confused when consequences for a particular type of behavior change from one episode to the next.

20
Sexuality

A four-year-old whose mother was expecting a baby wondered what the baby's sex would be. The child said, "We'll just have to wait until the baby comes out." Her mother asked, "How will we know then? Will it have a pink or blue blanket?" "Of course not!" replied the child. "We'll see if it has long hair or short hair."

GOD CREATED US male and female. Our sexuality is a gift from God, and it is good. Sexuality is a basic part of the human personality. It is present in children as well as in adults, in celibate persons as well as in those who are sexually active, in the elderly and infirm as well as in healthy young people. Sexuality begins when life begins, and its development is a gradual, lifelong process. Education in sexuality begins at birth, whether or not someone intentionally focuses on teaching it.

Sexuality Is Influenced by Example

In your efforts to help your child form a strong and healthy self-concept, you will also be shaping his or her sexuality. It is an essential part of the development of a sense of personal uniqueness. Part of learning about self includes learning about one's own body, about what it means to be a boy or girl, man or woman, about how life is created, about the various forms of intimacy as expressions of love and affection.

Much of your child's early education in sexuality, as in everything else, will be learned from you. The way you touch and hold your son or daughter, the way you respond to his or her curiosity about himself or herself or others, the way you relate to your spouse—all provide learning experiences which strongly influence your child's development of attitudes about sexuality.

It is important to be aware of and to understand your own attitudes, the things about which you are either comfortable or uncomfortable. If you are bothered by feelings of guilt or embarrassment about your own sexuality, you may want to consider sorting out these feelings with a competent helper so that you can avoid passing on the same attitudes to your child. Whether you deal with the topic openly or not, you are providing education in sexuality to your child day by day. Understanding your own attitudes will help you to communicate what you want your child to learn.

The greatest influence on your child's attitudes is clearly your personal example. There are, however, many other influences, and it is impossible to shield children from them totally. The media are full of messages about sexuality. Even cartoons and family-viewing television programs contain them. So do magazines and newspapers. Your child is going to come in contact with attitudes toward sexuality through friends and in the homes of relatives.

Because your influence in the early years is greater than any of these sources, you must use it to make certain that the values your child acquires toward sexuality are the ones you want him or her to have. The only way you can do this is by taking an active part—answering questions, discussing attitudes, and providing the kind of example you want your child to imitate. Your teaching needs to take place now because now is the time your child is learning and now is the time when your influence is the greatest.

Patterns of Development

Even during infancy the child is becoming aware of his or her own body. Just as each child discovers fingers, toes, and hair, he or she will discover genitals. This exploration is normal and healthy. As the child advances from infant to toddler, the interest in bodily discovery broadens into curiosity about other bodies. With so much similarity these days in clothing, hairstyles, and toys for little boys and girls, the difference in genitals is about the only difference little children can observe about each other. Noticing this difference is a part of the normal process by which a child gains self-identity as a "boy" or a "girl." So, when siblings who bathe together, or preschoolers who use the same bathroom, notice differences in anatomy and start asking questions, answer their questions openly and honestly. If the curiosity is satisfied now, it is not likely to be a problem later.

The manner in which toilet training is handled is also important to the development of healthy sexuality. Children who are made to feel embarrassed and ashamed of their bodily functions, especially those closely associated with being male or female, will find it difficult to accept their sexual identity. Start toilet training only when you are sure your child is ready for it; don't start just because you are tired of diapers. In toilet training, be lavish with praise; avoid shaming or punishing your child for accidents.

As children reach the older preschool level, they begin to show an interest in reproduction. Usually, their curiosity is centered around the growth of a baby in the womb and how the baby is born. They may need to be told that it takes both a man and a woman to make a baby. Generally, they will not show an interest at this time in the process by which conception occurs. But they are still very interested in physical differences and should be encouraged to use the correct names for parts of the body.

They may also begin to display a need for privacy while bathing or using the bathroom. Although this usually does not occur until six or seven, it should be respected whenever it is expressed.

Some Further Points

Your child's need to develop and to express her or his own sexual identity includes establishing respect for the rights of others. Curiosity about sexual identity does not give a child the right to violate another's need for privacy. For example, questions about reproduction need not be answered at a social gathering. Curiosity about body parts does not mean that a child can undress in the living room.

Children need to know that sexuality is good. They also need to learn that there are appropriate times, places, and ways of expressing sexuality. You can suggest acceptable options by saying things like "You need to stay in your room if you aren't dressed" to inform the child that it is OK to be nude but that there is a place for nudity. By saying things like "Let's find a picture that shows what a woman's body looks like" you communicate that it is all right to be curious even though Aunt Jane doesn't want to be peered at while she is in the bathtub.

Answer your child's questions as simply as possible. If you are comfortable with the discussion, your son or daughter will ask for more information when he or she wants it. Do not overwhelm with lengthy explanations. A child can absorb only a little at a time. Use the correct terminology. Children hear and use slang, but they should know the proper words for the parts of the body.

Achieving mature sexuality is one aspect of your child's unique personal development as part of God's plan.

21
Special Needs

Just as I was getting ready to swim out, the Lord tapped me on the shoulder... "Travis, I have a special assignment for you! You are going to be a very special little boy whom I'm going to use to touch and bless the lives of many people....Be assured I am going to help you....I'm giving you to people who love me and know me through Christ....I want you to go out there and remind people that I love them no matter how different they may be and for them to love each other!"...So folks, here I am...I'm excited to be alive...excited to share God's message of love. I need your help...treat me like any other little boy. I love you.

EXCERPTS FROM THE BIRTH ANNOUNCEMENT OF TRAVIS JOHN, WHO WAS BORN WITH DOWN SYNDROME

EVERY CHILD IS A GIFT, a manifestation of God's love, and every life is of value to God. But welcoming a child with special needs can be a difficult experience for parents.

During the image-making stage of parenting, you form a mental picture of the child you will have. You imagine a boy or a girl who will, of course, be attractive, intelligent, charming, athletic, and so on. Your baby will always be content and will smile a lot. Everyone will feel that you are lucky indeed to have such a delightful offspring.

But what happens if the child of your imaginings turns out to be a baby with limitations and/or problems—a baby with a cleft palate, mental handicaps, deformed limbs, deafness, or blindness? What if the baby has health difficulties, such as prematurity or a heart defect?

The birth of such a baby is usually greeted with sadness and regret. Friends and relatives are not sure whether they should offer congratulations or sympathy. They feel awkward and uncomfortable. The parents are disillusioned by a sense of failure to produce a healthy, "normal" child.

Parents of a baby with special needs usually experience feelings similar to the feelings they would have if a loved one had died—shock, denial, anger, guilt—all of which are normal feelings in the process of grieving for the loss of the healthy baby they were expecting. And as they endure this gamut of feelings, they must also learn to accept the real child who is now part of their lives.

Seeing and welcoming Christ and the Father in a child is the privilege and responsibility of parents, whether the child is disabled or not. Every child is a valued gift of God.

Again—the Importance of Self-Esteem

Developing a sense of worth and uniqueness is important to a child with special needs, perhaps more so than to other children. This child experiences many difficulties. The confidence and determination that stem from a sense of being valued and accepted are a tremendous support to a child who must cope with extraordinary challenges.

Sometimes a child with special needs makes others more aware of how unique a child is. As a child with certain limitations struggles to walk or to speak, those around him can begin to appreciate how much effort and skill these seemingly easy accomplishments require. The result is a new comprehension of every child's struggle for mastery of basic developmental tasks.

This child especially needs to learn about and to experience God's unconditional love. Being accepted with "no strings attached"—accepted for being rather than doing—is especially important and meaningful to children who will often be unable to compete successfully with others for achievement and recognition. The ability to understand religious concepts may be affected by such disabilities as mental handicaps. But every child can be made aware of God's care and love for each of us as unique parts of his creation. The ability of parents to accept a child's handicap provides tangible evidence of God's unconditional love. Parents who are able to accept their child with a disability are more likely to have a child who accepts himself. Parents need to communicate this sentiment through words or action: "We accept you the way you are. We are here to help you do the best with what God has given you." The child will then feel supported to accept himself. Parental love and acceptance will also provide an example for others.

Discipline Is Important

A disabled child's behavior may be blamed on his disability when, in fact, it is just a normal stage of development or the result of a lack of discipline. Sometimes parents feel sorry for their child or assume he cannot learn acceptable behavior. Such an attitude can magnify the child's problems and affect his development more than the disability itself.

When there are other children in the family, it can be difficult to meet everyone's needs. For example, some brain-damaged children are disruptive, and they disregard the rights of siblings. There are families who sacrifice the enjoyment of having a Christmas tree because their hyperactive child pulls the ornaments off or knocks the tree down. Some families forgo vacations and outings because such activities are difficult for their handicapped child to handle. Parents need to minimize the burden of such situations by taking whatever measures they can. For example, perhaps the handicapped child can stay with a relative while the rest of the family goes to a movie. Locks on the door may be necessary to safeguard privacy or to protect valued possessions. In such cases, the needs and rights of all family members must be considered. When compromises are necessary, the decision should not always be in favor of any one individual.

Children can learn patience, tolerance, and unselfishness from their experiences with a handicapped sibling. But they can also become angry and resentful. They may feel that their parents are overprotecting the child with special needs—at their expense. They may come to view him as a burden and make him the scapegoat when problems surface.

Support Is Available

A child with a special needs can increase the amount of stress in family relationships. Often there are additional expenses for medical needs, education, and counseling. Unresolved questions about the child's problems, progress, and future can cause parental anxiety. It can be difficult to find a baby-sitter when parents want to enjoy an evening out.

Critical family members and neighbors may contribute to parents' feelings of guilt and inadequacy. It is because of such factors that the breakup rate of families with a handicapped child is higher than the rate for the general population.

Today there is much support for families with handicapped children. One of the best forms of support comes from other parents who have been or are in similar situations. Organizations of such parents exist in most communities. Medical, educational, psychological, and financial support services are readily available today to help families with handicapped children. School districts are required to provide educational services beginning in the preschool years and, in some cases, during infancy. Many excellent books dealing with a variety of handicaps are available for parents and children. Finally, it is important that you, the parent, have some time for yourself and time to focus on the other members of the family.

To a child with special needs, the most important thing is to be accepted and treated as a child. First of all, this person is a child. The disability comes second.

22
Media

With a little skip in his step three-year-old Benjamin belted out a tune at the top of his lungs, "Oh, do you know the Spiderman who lives on Drury Lane?"

IN THIS BEAUTIFUL yet complicated world exists a parallel universe we call the media. This is a world we may try to ignore but can never deny. There is a great concern today among educators and child psychologists about the influence the media have on children. The most influential of the media is television. But radio, books, the Internet, magazines, and newspapers also influence children. All of these media come right into your home; they are part of the environment in which your child will grow up.

The influence of the media, especially television, is not always good. But if you approve of unhealthy media offerings—either directly by word or example or indirectly by allowing them to be there—your child is going to think that you find them acceptable.

The Good News and the Bad News

A great deal of attention has been given in recent years to the negative influence of television. It has been described as habit-forming and compared to addictive drugs. It has been deplored because of the violence and sex, the shallow values, the half-truths to which it exposes children.

These concerns about television are legitimate. But they are only half the picture. Television can also be a healthy influence on the development of children. It can educate them, entertain them, and help clarify their values. It can generate meaningful discussions within the family. The responsibility of parents is to make television a good and useful influence in the home.

The same can be said for other forms of media. Books, for example, can be powerful aids in helping children understand their world. By hearing stories about other children who have coped with such events in their lives, a child can learn to deal with the experience of a new baby, divorce, hospitalization, moving, death, and many other life experiences. A four-year-old boy, anxious about his first visit to the dentist, can be reassured by a book describing the procedures and equipment used in a dentist's office.

So—What's a Person to Do?

These are elements which you, as a parent, must try to control. How do you want TV-watching to affect your child? How much of it is good? While watching television, what are the messages the child is getting? Is TV a teacher or a convenient baby-sitter? Or is it both?

The first consideration must be the total amount of time your child spends watching television. Many programs, such as Sesame Street, are excellent for children. But young children need to be active in order to learn. They need to fill the dump truck with sand, count the forks that will be put on the table, talk to Mom about the butterfly in the yard, and argue with their friends about whose turn it is to ride a tricycle.

The passive nature of TV-watching interferes with such active learning experiences. Because of this most experts recommend no more than one hour of television per day for preschool children, regardless of the kind of programming to which they are exposed.

The violence which is so common on many television programs is another area of concern. Studies show that there is far more violence during children's programming than on prime-time shows. Cartoons are filled with violence. Children lack the experience to distinguish what is real from what is imaginary. It is perfectly believable for their favorite cartoon hero to be flattened by a steamroller, blown up by dynamite, and thrown off a cliff—all without suffering any permanent damage. Therefore, they become less sensitive to the tragedies which actually occur and are likely to react to them with indifference.

The tendency of children to believe what they see also affects the extent to which they are influenced by advertising on television. They believe that one kind of bread will give them bigger bodies, that mouthwash brings romance, and that "real" men drink a particular kind of beer. They do not understand that the purpose of a commercial is to sell a product.

Turning TV into a Positive Influence

The important practical question is: What can you as a parent do so that TV will have a positive influence on your child? Do you provide a model for other leisure activities such as reading, outdoor activities, crafts, and other hobbies? If you can help your child develop an early interest in and appreciation for such things, his or her tendency to rely on television will diminish.

Watch TV with your child, when possible, so you can point out things he or she does not understand, or explain if he or she has questions. Encourage your child to question what she sees—the motives, the results, the alternatives, etc.

Provide other experiences for your child. The more first-hand experiences he or she has, the less influence TV will have. Provide opportunities to counter the claims of advertising. Examine the product at the store to see if it really is better.

Talk about the difference between "real" and "pretend," and help your child to make the distinction. Finding out that TV families are "pretend families" is often a big surprise to children. Once they realize that these actors are playing a part, children will understand that what the actors are doing is "pretend."

Sometimes you can point out how the illusions on TV are created—that people do not really fly, knock each other out, sit in a car that goes off a cliff, see through walls, and so on.

The forms of media you select for your home and family

should be consistent with your goals. The Catholic family should demonstrate Christian values in every aspect of life. The kinds and quality of media in your home are an important part of the environment of your domestic Church.

23
Technology and Communication

Three-year-old Sean kneeled in his father's chair and furiously pounded away on the computer keys, the whole while squinting his eyes at the screen with a very intense expression. His mother asked him what he was doing, and he replied, "I'm trying to get my e-mail out."

THOUGH TECHNOLOGY is much more of an issue for parents of teenagers and even pre-teens, it is still something that parents of young children should pay attention to in the early years of a child's life.

The reality is that many children under the age of six are using the computer today; it not the foreign object that it was for many of the parents at that age. A toddler will pick up a cell phone and hold it to his ear and mimic his father. A four-year-old believes he can't watch TV if the remote is lost. A three- or four-year-old knows how to gain access to the internet. We can't ignore the difference in upbringing our children will have with even more and more technological innovations popping up each day.

So what does this all mean to your young child?

The Good, the Bad, and the Ugly

The Good

The computer and other forms of technology have both good and bad ramifications in the development of a young child. So many wonderful programs have been developed to help a young child learn. The schools today are incorporating computer use into almost all aspects of curriculum.

For a young child, these experiences are all an excellent way to prepare them for a future job and life which will more than likely be one with a great deal of technology.

The Bad

When one mother saw the confused look on her daughter's face as she looked at the cord and the rotary dial of the phone at Grandma's house, she knew that a huge gap existed between this little girl's world and the one she knew as a young child.

This gap means that many still live in the old world and resent the present onslaught of technological gimmicks and conveniences. Parents need to attempt to bridge the gap for a developing young mind. When children grow accustomed to computer games, they need to be reminded of the wonder that can come from an empty box or crayons. A major concern is that young children who spend too much time in the "techno" world may have a very difficult time learning to be resourceful and think for themselves.

The Ugly

In extreme cases, technology can be very detrimental to your young child. If unmonitored, a child may encounter frightening and overwhelming experiences in certain computer games and PlayStation™ games. Violence and sex are present in many games that are marked unsuitable for young children. If a young child feels comfortable being alone at the computer, he or she may develop into an older child whose curiosity, unmonitored, might lead him to dangerous interactions on the Internet.

Finally, we must use caution in warning our children of the dangers of some forms of technology. One little boy shared with his mother what his friend had told him at preschool. "Zach said that he heard about a kid in Japan who did so much PlayStation™ that his brain exploded all over the TV."

Parents will need to balance the good, the bad and the ugly in talking with a young child about technology. Again, parents will especially need to monitor the child and the amount of time he or she spends on different forms of technology.

But what does all of this information on technology have to do with the faith of your child?

Just how can technology impact the faith of your child? Communication is greatly impacted by the overuse or misuse of technology. Part of God's plan for our time on earth is for us to experience joy of wonder, curiosity, and human interaction. Ultimately, our communication with God can be avoided if we focus too much on virtual communication day in and day out. Parents of young children can guide them to focus and remind them of our purpose in the world.

24
Living in a Material World

At Emma's third birthday, she sat like a queen in a big chair in the living room as she opened presents from all of the friends and family who had come to help her celebrate such a significant milestone. After throwing on the floor the wrapping paper from the gift she had just opened, she looked around the room and asked, "OK, now who else wants to give me a present?"

TO MANY FORTUNATE PEOPLE, the world is a very comfortable and luxurious place. Many are so blessed today as they live a lifestyle which others today and many before them could only dream about. A world without basic needs is beyond their realm of thought. Because many in the materialistic world have known nothing but this lifestyle, they may unknowingly ignore the reality of others.

As adults, we know this. Still, the smile on a child's face when he or she receives a gift is one of the greatest moments to a mother or father. Christmas, birthdays and other special events are great opportunities for those "moments." Soon grandparents, extended family, and friends want to jump in on the moments, and eventually a child grows to expect the gifts. Sometimes they want things even when there is no occasion.

The domino effect of gift-giving spirals from the best of intentions. The result in the end is not always good. Stan and Jan Berenstain spell this out beautifully in their book The Berenstain Bears Get the Gimmies. When the young cubs become bratty and demanding, Mother Bear and Father Bear turn to their own parents to complain. The parents sigh that they can't go anywhere without the kids crying "Gimmie." But the "grand-bears" point to the role that Mother Bear and Father Bear had in their children getting such a bad case of the gimmies.

A world with many "things" can skew our perspective on what our purpose is in this world. So what does this mean to a young child today? And just what can a parent do to counteract the materialist world and our own materialistic tendencies? Parents must work hard to balance the material world in which we live with a sincere and spiritual approach to the life that God has so graciously given us.

A grateful heart and loving spirit can be the best response to the fortunate world we create for our children. Repeated discussions with children about how blessed we are in our comfort does make a difference. Praying for the less fortunate every day and talking about specific situations of people not as comfortable creates compassion in children that can only be learned from loving parents.

In Luke 12:48, Jesus explains to a servant, "Everyone to whom much has been given, much will be required; and from the one to whom much has been entrusted, even more will be demanded." A daily reminder to even a very young child of this message along with the specifics will prove valuable. One mother tells her young daughter, "Because we are so lucky to have food on our tables each day, we are going to help our parish deliver Meals on Wheels to the older people in our community who can't get out to get food." A child learns quickly to "give" and minister as he or she is placed in many giving situations.

How do we help children focus on Christ in the midst of such great materialism? We certainly can't change the way the world runs right at this moment, but we can keep a constant dialogue going on with our children, especially young children.

To those who have been given much, much will be expected. To the parent who has been so blessed to receive the gift of this very special child from the Lord, much will be expected in this holy calling as mother or father to the child.

25
Death

Death is not extinguishing the light,
but putting out the lamp because the dawn has come.

RABINDRANATH TAGORE

IN THE CHRISTIAN FAMILY death brings a mingling of grief and sadness, hope and joy. We mourn the loss of a loved one and celebrate his or her transition to eternal life. By your example you can teach your child that death is not only an ending but also a beginning, one which is shared through faith by all Christians.

The concept of death is difficult for a small child to understand. Until a child has had some experience with death through the loss of a grandparent, friend, or a beloved pet, death is just a word. For instance, a child who was told that she couldn't walk up a particular street because there was a dead end there responded, "Well, can't we just step over it?"

Little children are as curious about death as they are about everything else in their world. They observe dead birds and insects with great fascination. They shoot each other in "battle" and "die" when they play hospital. They come right back to life, of course, unable to understand the finality of death. However, unlike most adults, they are not reluctant to talk about death.

Much of this lack of fear is due to the child's inability to appreciate the gravity of death or his or her own mortality. From birth through age five, the child, due to an immature concept of time, cannot grasp the permanence of death. A child sees death as a separation, but not one which is final.

As the child becomes older (ages six through nine), a realization develops that death is permanent, but it is perceived as something that happens to people when they get old. Not until later (age ten) does the child discover his or her own mortality, and that is the point at which the meaning of death should be dealt with. Until that time most children cannot envision their home or family continuing to exist without their presence. They are still the center of their world, and death is something that happens only to others.

Discuss Death Openly

Learning about death should be a gradual process, as with any other area of learning. Your child's questions should be answered honestly and simply. Protecting your child from knowledge about death and shielding him or her from things that are painful may be a natural desire for you. However, if you give information when your child expresses an interest and readiness for it, you will be handling the topic in the best possible way.

Often, adults do not openly discuss death because it is hard for them, not hard for the child. If you do have a difficulty, there are several excellent books for little children that deal with the topic of death. Nature is also an excellent teacher; a dead bug or goldfish can provide a good firsthand experience as well as an opportunity for discussion. The best way to teach is to take advantage of natural lessons as they occur.

If your family is affected by the death of a relative or friend, allow your child to share in the experience of grieving. Protecting your child from a painful reality or preventing the child from seeing you vulnerable in your own grief can actually cause fear and anxiety in the child. The child senses something wrong but feels isolated from what is happening. The extent of involvement should depend on the child's own feelings, but the opportunity to participate should be made available. Your child needs to be included, with the understanding that he or she is not expected to do anything but may be involved if she or he wishes.

This extends to wakes and funerals: Again, the child should participate in the decision regarding his or her involvement. It can be damaging to a child to be left with a friend while the rest of the family attend Grandma's funeral. Children need the opportunity to say good-bye to a loved one just as adults do. Simply explain the situation to the child to the best of your ability, and then let the child decide what he or she is comfortable with. For example, do not force the child to view the body against his or her will, because that can have lasting negative consequences.

Christian Belief Makes Death Easier to Accept

For Christians and others who believe in eternal life, death is easier to accept and to explain. Even though they cannot grasp it, small children can be told that every person has a body and a spirit (or soul) and that at death the body dies but the spirit continues to live. A child can more readily accept separation from a loved one through death and burial if he or she knows that a part of the person continues to live.

Be careful how you tell a child that Grandpa's soul is happy with God in heaven; the child may wonder why Grandpa had to go to heaven to be happy. To child-logic, the conclusion is that something or someone on earth made Grandpa unhappy. It might be better to explain that Grandpa's body was too sick (or too old or too hurt) for him to use it anymore, so his spirit left his body and is now in heaven. The important points to share with your child are that we have a body and soul, that the body and soul live together on earth for a while, and then the soul goes to heaven.

If your child asks, give as accurate an explanation as you can of the reason for death. You might say, "Grandma's heart was worn out." It is not a good idea to tell a child that a dead person is asleep. The child might think that sleep and death are similar and become afraid of going to sleep.

Children Grieve in Their Own Way

You must not be surprised if your child does not grieve as you would, even at the death of a family member. An eight-year-old told his pastor, "The funniest thing happened last night. My mom had a baby and it died." A six-year-old girl whose father died was delighted to see the relatives arrive for the funeral, thinking only of the fun of playing with her cousins.

This does not mean that these children are insensitive. The little girl loved her father deeply and grieved at his death, but she was a child and reacted as a child. The full impact of the loss simply could not be understood at the time.

Children need to be encouraged to express their sense of loss in ways meaningful to them. A child may say, "Now who will play ball with me?" He or she is expressing awareness that a person is gone. This is what the individual meant to the child, what he or she has lost.

Keeping the memory of loved ones alive is important to children. You can help by showing your child pictures of the person and recalling things that were special about the loved one. You might say, "Grandpa used to enjoy the roses so much." This helps the child realize that the person who died is still to be remembered as a part of life.

Be Truthful and Be Sensitive to a Child's Needs

Accepting your own feelings of grief is just as important as accepting your child's. Children are sensitive to what is going on around them; it is upsetting to them, when they know there is a problem, to be told "Go play." It is better for you to explain that you are crying because someone has died and you feel sad. Now your child knows why you are upset. He or she also knows that it is OK to feel sad and to cry when someone dies.

Children will often imagine things that are far worse than the truth if they do not have all the information they need. Cases like this really happen: a father dies of a heart attack, and his little boy blames himself because he made Daddy angry by not picking up his toys.

The comments people make can also affect a child's thinking. When a child has lost a mother, comments like "Having that last baby ruined her health" can be devastating and can cause needless guilt. It is things like this that make it especially important for you to encourage your child to talk about his or her perception of death. Then you can correct mistaken conclusions or inaccurate information.

In the Christian family, death is an ending and also a beginning. It is by your example that you teach this to your child.

A Final Word

Remember that you are the domestic Church. The guidance and strength you need to be a good parent are available to you through God's help; God is your co-parent. Many resources are available, simply waiting for you to take advantage of them. The role of the family within the Church is being emphasized, and there are books, periodicals, programs, and organizations to help you and your family find a way to grow spiritually.

Remember that you have been called. Take advantage of the opportunities, and you will find a way to participate which is spiritually meaningful. Let your parish know your needs so that your Church can respond to them. Become involved in your parish and share your strengths with others.

Remember that you are holy. The development of your child's faith is rooted in family experiences during the early years of childhood. In order to become spiritually strong and alive, your child must find a living faith through you and your family, the "Church in the Home."

About the Authors

Phyllis Chandler, a mother of four and a grandmother, has spent forty years working in the field of early childhood education and family life. She holds a B.A. and M.A. in Human Development and is a writer and consultant for the Omaha Catholic Archdiocese.

Joan Burney, a farmwife and mother of six, is an award-winning writer, lecturer, and TV commentator. A cum laude graduate of Mount Marty College in South Dakota, Mrs. Burney has completed her Ph.D. in psychology.

Mary Kay Leatherman, a mother of three, is a published author and an award-winning teacher. She holds a B.A. in English and Secondary Education from Creighton University and has worked with a number of baptism and spiritual parenting programs in several different communities.

Additional
Readings

Becoming Parents

Chapman, Gary. The Five Love Languages. Northfield Publishing, 1995.

Driscoll, Daniel W. Daddyhood: This Changes Everything.

Favaro, Dr. Peter. Smart Parenting: An Easy Approach to Raising Happy, Well-Adjusted Kids, Ages 2-12. Contemporary Books Inc., 1995.

Gottman, John M., Ph.D. and Nan Silver. The Seven Principles of Making Marriage Work. Crown Publishers, Inc. N.Y. 1999.

Hart, Kathleen and Thomas. Promises to Keep. Paulist Press. 1991.

Healy, Dr. James. When the Cake is Gone: How to Get Married and Stay Engaged. A forty five minute talk on CD.

Otto, Donna. Finding Your Purpose as a Mom: How to Build Your Home on Holy Ground. Harvest House Publisher. 2004.

Being a Family

Coloroso, Barbara. Parenting with Wit and Wisdom in Times of Chaos and Loss. Penguin Group, Viking. 1999.

Covey, Stephen. The 7 Habits of Highly Effective Families. Golden Books, N.Y. 1997.

Curran, Dolores. Traits of a Healthy Family. Winston Press. 1983.

Doherty, William J., Ph.D. Take Your Kids Back: Confident Parenting in Turbulent Times. Sorin Books. Notre Dame, Indiana. 2000.

Power, Thomas A., ACSW. Family Matters: A Layman's Guide to Family Functioning. Hathaway Press. 1989.

Wesselman. The Whole Parent: How to Become a Terrific Parent Even if You Didn't Have One. Insight Books, N.Y. 1998.

Being a Catholic Family

Gurian, Michael. The Soul of the Child: Nurturing the Divine Identity of Our Children. Atria Books, N.Y. 2002.

Hahn, Kimberly. Generation to Generation: Nurturing the Faith in Our Homes. Benedictus Books. 2005.

Hendricksen, Mary Lynn and Cathy O'Connell-Cahill. At Home With Our Faith. Spirituality Newsletter for Families. 1-800-328-6515.

Kritenbrink, Cynthia, Laura Baum-Parr and Mary Jo Pedersen. Welcome Your Child: Family Enrichment at Baptism and Beyond. The Archdiocese of Omaha. 2000.

Leach, Michael and Theresa Borchard. I Like Being Catholic: Treasured Traditions, Rituals and Stories. Doubleday.

Meehan, Bridget, SSC. D. Min. Creating a Loving Family: A Practical Handbook for Catholic Parents. Liguori Publication. 1992.

O'Connell-Chesto, Kathleen. Why are the Dandelions Weeds? Liguori. 1999.

Raising Children in Today's World

Buddenberg, Laura J. and Kathleen M. McGee. Who's Raising Your Child? Battling the Marketers for Your Child's Heart and Soul. Boys Town Press. 2004.

Coloroso, Barbara. Kids are Worth It! : Giving Your Child the Gift of Inner Discipline. Avon Books, N.Y. 1994.

Dinkmeyer, Don, PH.D. and Gary D. McKay, PH.D., STEP: Systematic Training for Effective Parenting of Children under Six. American Guidance Service 1989.

Eyre, Linda and Richard. Teaching Your Children Values. Fireside Books, N.Y. 1993.

McGinnis, Kathleen and James. Parenting for Peace and Justice: Ten Years Later. Orbis Books, N.Y. 1990.

Steyer, James P. The Other Parent: The Inside Story of the Media's Effect on our Children. Atria Books, N.Y. 2002.

CPSIA information can be obtained
at www.ICGtesting.com
Printed in the USA
FSOW02n2316310117
30116FS

9 780764 815232